FREE DVD   FREE   FREE DVD

From Stress to Success DVD from Trivium Test Prep

Dear Customer,

Thank you for purchasing from Trivium Test Prep! Whether you're a new teacher or looking to advance your career, we're honored to be a part of your journey.

To show our appreciation (and to help you relieve a little of that test-prep stress), we're offering a **FREE** *ACT Test Tips DVD** by Trivium Test Prep. Our DVD includes 35 test preparation strategies that will help keep you calm and collected before and during your big exam. All we ask is that you email us your feedback and describe your experience with our product. Amazing, awful, or just so-so: we want to hear what you have to say!

To receive your **FREE** *ACT Test Tips DVD*, please email us at 5star@triviumtestprep. com. Include "Free 5 Star" in the subject line and the following information in your email:

1. The title of the product you purchased.
2. Your rating from 1 – 5 (with 5 being the best).
3. Your feedback about the product, including how our materials helped you meet your goals and ways in which we can improve our products.
4. Your full name and shipping address so we can send your **FREE** *ACT Test Tips DVD*.

If you have any questions or concerns please feel free to contact us directly at 5star@triviumtestprep.com.

Thank you, and good luck with your studies!

* Please note that the free DVD is <u>not included</u> with this book. To receive the free DVD, please follow the instructions above.

ACT Prep Book 2018-2019

2018-2019

ACT Study Guide and Practice Test Questions for the ACT Test

TABLE OF CONTENTS

INTRODUCTION

Congratulations on choosing the take the ACT! By purchasing this book, you've taken the first step toward getting accepted by the college of your choice.

This guide will provide you with a detailed overview of the ACT so you know exactly what to expect on test day. We'll take you through all the concepts covered on the test and give you the opportunity to test your knowledge with practice questions. Even if you're nervous about taking such a big test, don't worry; we'll make sure you're more than ready!

What is the ACT?

The ACT is an achievement test designed to assess what you've learned in school. Universities will look at your ACT score to help determine if you're ready to tackle college-level material. However, your test score won't be the only thing that schools look at; they'll also consider your high school transcript, letters of recommendations, and school activities. So, while the ACT is an important part of your college application, it's only one part of the application process.

What's on the ACT?

The ACT consists of five sections: English, mathematics, reading, science, and writing. The first four sections are multiple-choice; the writing section requires you to write a short expository essay. The writing section is optional and will not affect your composite score; however, some colleges will require a writing sample score. You should decide when you register for the test whether you want to take this portion.

SECTION	CONCEPTS	NUMBER OF QUESTIONS	TIME
English	identifying errors in basic grammar, punctuation, usage, and style; rhetorical skills	75 questions	45 minutes
Mathematics	performing calculations using numbers and operations, algebra, geometry, and basic statistics	60 questions	60 minutes
Reading	understanding and analyzing non-fiction and fiction passages; vocabulary in context	40 questions	35 minutes
Science	interpreting scientific passages, experiments, and data	40 questions	35 minutes
Writing	crafting a clear, well-written essay	1 prompt	40 minutes

How is the ACT Scored?

You'll receive a point for every correctly answered multiple-choice question. There is no penalty for incorrect answers. The number of correctly answered questions becomes your raw score, which is then scaled to a score from 1 to 36. Your composite score is the average of your scaled score on each of the four multiple-choice sections.

The writing section will not affect your composite score. Two graders will score your essay from 1 to 6 in four domains: ideas and analysis, development and support, organization, and language use and conventions. Your summed scores for each of these domains will be included on your score report. The graders' scores will also be scaled to create an overall writing score from 1 to 36.

How is the ACT Administered?

The ACT is a paper-based test available at testing centers around the U.S. and the world. Refer to the ACT website for testing dates and sites.

On the day of your test, arrive early and be sure to bring proper identification and your admission ticket (which is emailed to you after you register). You are required to put away all personal belongings before the test begins. Cell phones and other electronic, photographic, recording, or listening devices are not permitted in the testing center at all. You are allowed pencils, erasers, and a four-function or scientific calculator on your desk during the test. Calculators may only be used for the mathematics section. A watch that will not sound during the test is also allowed. For details on what to expect on testing day, refer to the ACT website.

About This Guide

This guide will help you to master the most important test topics and also develop critical test-taking skills. We have built features into our books to prepare you for your tests and increase your score. Along with a detailed summary of the test's format, content, and scoring, we offer an in-depth overview of the content knowledge required to pass the test. In the review you'll find sidebars that provide interesting information, highlight key concepts, and review content so that you can solidify your understanding of the exam's concepts. You can also test your knowledge with sample questions throughout the text and practice questions that reflect the content and format of the ACT. We're pleased you've chosen Accepted, Inc. to be a part of your journey!

PART I: REVIEW

one

ENGLISH

75 questions ¦ 45 minutes

The English section consists of five passages. Various parts of the passages will be underlined, and the corresponding multiple choice questions will ask you to improve the underlined portion or leave it as it is. The questions will test your understanding of the basic rules of grammar, punctuation, spelling, and capitalization. Some of the topics you might see include:

◆ matching pronouns with their antecedents

◆ matching verbs with their subjects

◆ ensuring that verbs are in the correct tense

◆ placing modifying phrases correctly

◆ correcting sentences for parallel construction

◆ maintaining point of view within a sentence

◆ organizing sentences within paragraphs

◆ adding and deleting sentences

English Strategies

Don't just check the grammar. The writers of the ACT consider the best choice to be the one which is most concise while still being complete. The correct answer will use the least number of words possible while still using proper English. You can eliminate answer choices that contain

◆ redundancies (multiple words that mean the same things)

◆ irrelevancies (words or ideas not directly or logically associated with the main idea)

◆ wordiness (words that may be grammatically correct but which do not add meaning to the sentence)

Read every word of every question. Don't assume you know what is being asked after reading the first few words. Remember, one word at the end of a sentence can change its entire meaning.

Read all the answer choices before making a selection. Some choices will be partially correct (pertaining to a part, but not all, of the passage) and are intended to catch the eye of the sloppy tester. Note the differences between your answer choices; sometimes they are very subtle.

Familiarize yourself with various styles of writing. The ACT passages can be cause/effect essays, comparison/contrast essays, definition essays, description essays, narration essays, persuasive essays, or process analysis essays.

Practice using the real test format. The format of the English section can be confusing for many test-takers, so practice answering similarly formatted test questions before test day.

Know the test directions. Knowing the directions before test day saves valuable minutes. It enables you to glance quickly at the directions and start answering questions.

STANDARD DIRECTIONS FOR THE ENGLISH SECTION

This test consists of five passages. In each passage, certain words and phrases have been underlined and numbered. The questions on each passage consist of alternatives for these underlined segments. Choose the alternative that follows standard written English, most accurately reflects the style and tone of the passage, or best relays the idea of the passage. Choose No Change if no change is necessary. You are to choose the best answer to the question.

You will also find questions about a section of the passage, or the passage as a whole. These questions do not refer to the underlined portions of the passage, but are identified by a boxed number. For each question, choose the alternative that best answers the question.

Parts of Speech

The first step in getting ready for this section of the test is to review parts of speech and the rules that accompany them. The good news is that you have been using these rules since you first began to speak; even if you don't know a lot of the technical terms, many of these rules may be familiar to you.

Nouns and Pronouns

NOUNS are people, places, or things. For example, in the sentence *The hospital was very clean*, the noun is hospital; it is a place. Pronouns replace nouns and make sentences sound less repetitive. Take the sentence *Sam stayed home from school because Sam was not feeling well*. The word *Sam* appears twice in the same sentence. To avoid repetition and improve the sentence, use a pronoun instead: *Sam stayed at home because he did not feel well*.

Because pronouns take the place of nouns, they need to agree both in number and gender with the noun they replace. So, a plural noun needs a plural pronoun, and a feminine noun needs a feminine pronoun. In the first sentence of this paragraph, for example, the plural pronoun *they* replaced the plural noun *pronouns*. There will usually be several questions on the English section of the ACT that cover pronoun agreement, so it's good to get comfortable spotting pronouns.

SINGULAR PRONOUNS
- I, me, mine, my
- you, your, yours
- he, him, his
- she, her, hers
- it, its

PLURAL PRONOUNS
- we, us, our, ours
- they, them, their, theirs

 EXAMPLES

Wrong: *If a student forgets their homework, it is considered incomplete.*

Correct: *If a student forgets his or her homework, it is considered incomplete.*

Student is a singular noun, but *their* is a plural pronoun, making the first sentence grammatically incorrect. To correct it, replace *their* with the singular pronoun *his* or *her*.

Wrong: *Everybody will receive their paychecks promptly.*

Correct: *Everybody will receive his or her paycheck promptly.*

Everybody is a singular noun, but *their* is a plural pronoun; the first sentence is grammatically incorrect. To correct it, replace *their* with the singular pronoun *his* or *her*.

Wrong: *When a nurse begins work at a hospital, you should wash your hands.*

Correct: *When a nurse begins work at a hospital, he or she should wash his or her hands.*

This sentence begins in third-person perspective and finishes in second-person perspective. To correct it, ensure the sentence finishes with third-person perspective.

Wrong: *After the teacher spoke to the student, she realized her mistake.*

Correct: *After Mr. White spoke to his student, she realized her mistake. (she and her referring to student)*

Correct: *After speaking to the student, the teacher realized her own mistake. (her referring to teacher)*

This sentence refers to a teacher and a student. But to whom does *she* refer, the teacher or the student? To improve clarity, use specific names or state more clearly who spotted the mistake.

Verbs

Remember the old commercial, *Verb: It's what you do*? That sums up verbs in a nutshell. A VERB is the action of a sentence: verbs *do* things. A verb must be conjugated to match the context of the sentence; this can sometimes be tricky because English has many irregular verbs. For example, *run* is an action verb in the present tense that becomes *ran* in the past tense; the linking verb *is* (which describes a state of being) becomes *was* in the past tense.

Table 1.1. Conjugation of the Verb *To Be*

	PAST	PRESENT	FUTURE
SINGULAR	was	is	will be
PLURAL	were	are	will be

Verb tense must make sense in the context of the sentence. For example, the sentence *I was baking cookies and eat some dough* probably sounds strange. That's because the two verbs *was baking* and *eat* are in different tenses. *Was baking* occurred in the past; *eat*, on the other hand, occurs in the present. To correct this error, conjugate *eat* in the past tense: *I was baking cookies and ate some dough.*

Like pronouns, verbs must agree in number with the noun they refer back to. In the example above, the verb *was* refers back to the singular *I*. If the subject of the sentence was plural, it would need to be modified to read *They were baking cookies and ate some dough*. Note that the verb *ate* does not change form; this is common for verbs in the past tense.

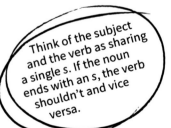

Think of the subject and the verb as sharing a single s. If the noun ends with an s, the verb shouldn't and vice versa.

 EXAMPLES

Wrong: *The cat chase the ball while the dogs runs in the yard.*

Correct: *The cat chases the ball while the dogs run in the yard.*

Cat is singular, so it takes a singular verb (which confusingly ends with an s); *dogs* is plural, so it needs a plural verb.

Wrong: *The cars that had been recalled by the manufacturer was returned within a few months.*

Correct: *The cars that had been recalled by the manufacturer were returned within a few months.*

Sometimes the subject and verb are separated by clauses or phrases. Here, the subject *cars* is separated from the verb phrase *were returned*, making it more difficult to conjugate the verb correctly; this results in a number error.

Correct: *The deer hid in the trees.*

Correct: *The deer are not all the same size.*

The subject of these sentences is a collective noun, which describes a group of people or things. This noun can be singular if it is referring to the group as a whole or plural if it refers to each item in the group as a separate entity.

Correct: *The doctor and nurse work in the hospital.*

Correct: *Neither the nurse nor her boss was scheduled to take a vacation.*

Correct: *Either the patient or her parents complete her discharge paperwork.*

When the subject contains two or more nouns connected by *and*, that subject is plural and requires a plural verb. Singular subjects joined by *or, either/or, neither/nor,* or *not only/but also* remain singular; when these words join plural and singular subjects, the verb should match the closest subject.

Wrong: *Because it will rain during the party last night, we had to move the tables inside.*

Correct: *Because it rained during the party last night, we had to move the tables inside.*

All the verb tenses in a sentence need to agree both with each other and with the other information in the sentence. In the first sentence above, the tense doesn't match the other information in the sentence: *last night* indicates the past (rained) not the future (will rain).

If the subject is separated from the verb, cross out the phrases between them to make conjugation easier.

Adjectives and Adverbs

ADJECTIVES are words that describe a noun. Take the sentence *The boy hit the ball.* If you want to know more about the noun *ball,* then you could use an adjective to describe him: *The boy hit the red ball.* An adjective simply provides more information about a noun in a sentence.

Like adjectives, ADVERBS provide more information about a part of a sentence. Adverbs can describe verbs, adjectives, and even other adverbs. For example, in the sentence *The doctor had recently hired a new employee,* the adverb *recently* tells us more about how the action *hired* took place. Often, but not always, adverbs end in *–ly.*

Remember that adverbs can never describe nouns—only adjectives can.

Adjectives, adverbs, and modifying phrases (groups of words that together modify another word) should always be placed as close as possible to the word they modify. Separating words from their modifiers can result in incorrect or confusing sentences.

 EXAMPLES

Wrong: *Running through the hall, the bell rang and the student knew she was late.*

Correct: *Running through the hall, the student heard the bell ring and knew she was late.*

The phrase *running through the hall* should be placed next to *student*, the noun it modifies.

Wrong: *The terrifyingly lion's loud roar scared the zoo's visitors.*

Correct: *The lion's terrifyingly loud roar scared the zoo's visitors.*

While the lion may indeed be terrifying, the word *terrifyingly* is an adverb and so can only modify a verb, an adjective or another adverb, not the noun *lion*. In the second sentence, *terrifyingly* is modifying the adjective *loud*, telling us more about the loudness of the lion's roar—so loud, it was terrifying.

Other Parts of Speech

Just a few other prepositions include after, between, by, during, of, on, to, and with.

PREPOSITIONS generally help describe relationships in space and time; they may express the location of a noun or pronoun in relation to other words and phrases in a sentence. For example, in the sentence *The nurse parked her car in a parking garage*, the preposition *in* describes the position of the car in relation to the garage. The noun that follows the preposition is called its *object*. In the example above, the object of the preposition *in* is the noun *parking garage*.

CONJUNCTIONS connect words, phrases, and clauses. The conjunctions summarized in the acronym FANBOYS—for, and, nor, but, or, yet, so—are called COORDINATING CONJUNCTIONS and are used to join independent clauses. For example, in the sentence *The nurse prepared the patient for surgery, and the doctor performed the surgery*, the conjunction *and* joins the two independent clauses together. SUBORDINATING CONJUNCTIONS, like *although, because,* and *if,* join together an independent and dependent clause. In the sentence *She had to ride the subway because her car was broken*, the conjunction *because* joins together the two clauses. (Independent and dependent clauses are covered in more detail below.)

INTERJECTIONS, like *wow* and *hey*, express emotion and are most commonly used in conversation and casual writing. They are often followed by *exclamation points*.

Constructing Sentences

Phrases and Clauses

A PHRASE is a group of words acting together that contain either a subject or verb, but not both. Phrases can be constructed from several different parts of speech. For example, a prepositional phrase includes a preposition and the object of that preposition (e.g., *under the table*), and a verb phrase includes the main verb and any helping verbs (e.g., *had been running*). Phrases cannot stand alone as sentences.

A CLAUSE is a group of words that contains both a subject and a verb. There are two types of clauses: INDEPENDENT CLAUSES can stand alone as sentences, and DEPENDENT CLAUSES cannot stand alone. Again, dependent clauses are recognizable as they begin with subordinating conjunctions.

 EXAMPLES

Classify each of the following as a phrase, independent clause, or dependent clause:

1. I have always wanted to drive a bright red sports car
2. under the bright sky filled with stars
3. because my sister is running late

Number 1 is an independent clause—it has a subject (*I*) and a verb (*have wanted*) and has no subordinating conjunction. **Number 2 is a phrase** made up of a preposition (*under*), its object (*sky*), and words that modify sky (*bright, filled with stars*), but lacks a conjugated verb. **Number 3 is a dependent clause**—it has a subject (*sister*), a verb (*is running*), and a subordinating conjunction (*because*).

Types of Sentences

A sentence can be classified as simple, compound, complex, or compound-complex based on the type and number of clauses it has.

GO ON

Table 1.2. Sentence Classification

Sentence Type	Number of Independent Clauses	Number of Dependent Clauses
simple	1	0
compound	2+	0
complex	1	1+
compound-complex	2+	1+

A SIMPLE SENTENCE consists of only one independent clause. Because there are no dependent clauses in a simple sentence, it can be as short as two words, a subject and a verb (e.g., *I ran.*). However, a simple sentence may also contain prepositions, adjectives, and adverbs. Even though these additions can extend the length of a simple sentence, it is still considered a simple sentence as long as it doesn't contain any dependent clauses.

COMPOUND SENTENCES have two or more independent clauses and no dependent clauses. Usually a comma and a coordinating conjunction (*for, and, nor, but, or, yet,* and *so*) join the independent clauses, though semicolons can be used as well. For example, the sentence *My computer broke, so I took it to be repaired* is compound.

COMPLEX SENTENCES have one independent clause and at least one dependent clause. In the complex sentence *If you lie down with dogs, you'll wake up with fleas,* the first clause is dependent (because of the subordinating conjunction if), and the second is independent.

COMPOUND-COMPLEX SENTENCES have two or more independent clauses and at least one dependent clause. For example, the sentence *City traffic frustrates David because the streets are congested, so he is seeking an alternate route home,* is compound-complex. *City traffic frustrates David* is an independent clause, as is *he is seeking an alternate route home*; however the subordinating conjunction *because* indicates that *because the streets are so congested* is a dependent clause.

 EXAMPLES

Classify: *San Francisco is one of my favorite places in the United States.*

Although the sentence is lengthy, it is **simple** because it contains only one subject and verb (*San Francisco... is*) modified by additional phrases.

Classify: *I love listening to the radio in the car because I enjoy loud music on the open road.*

The sentence has one independent clause (*I love... car*) and one dependent (*because I... road*), so it is **complex**.

Joining two independent clauses with only a comma and no coordinating conjunction is a punctuation error called a comma splice—be on the lookout for these.

Classify: *I wanted to get a dog, but I got a fish because my roommate is allergic to pet dander.*

This sentence has three clauses: two independent (*I wanted... dog* and *I got a fish*) and one dependent (*because my... dander*), so it is **compound-complex**.

Classify: *The game was cancelled, but we will still practice on Saturday.*

This sentence is made up of two independent clauses joined by a conjunction (*but*), so it is **compound**.

Clause Placement

In addition to the classifications above, sentences can also be defined by the location of the main clause. In a periodic sentence, the main idea of the sentence is held until the end. In a cumulative sentence, the independent clause comes first, and any modifying words or clauses follow it. (Note that this type of classification—periodic or cumulative—is not used in place of the simple, compound, complex, or compound-complex classifications. A sentence can be both cumulative and complex, for example.)

 EXAMPLES

Classify: *The GED, the TASC, the SAT, the ACT—this dizzying array of exams proved no match for the determined students.*

In this sentence the main independent clause—*this... students*—is held until the very end, so it's **periodic**. Furthermore, despite its length the sentence is **simple** because it has only one subject (*dizzying array*) and verb (*proved*).

Classify: *Jessica was well-prepared for the test, for she had studied for weeks, taken practice exams, and reviewed the material with other students.*

Here, the main clause *Jessica...test* begins the sentence; the other clauses modify the main clause, providing more information about the main idea and resulting in a **cumulative sentence**. In addition, the sentence is **compound** as it links two independent clauses together with a comma and the coordinating conjunction *for*.

Punctuation

The basic rules for using the major punctuation marks are given in the following table.

Table 1.3. Basic Punctuation Rules

Punctuation	Purpose	Example
period	ending sentences	Periods go at the end of complete sentences.
question mark	ending questions	What's the best way to end a sentence?
exclamation point	indicating interjections or commands; ending sentences that show extreme emotion	Help! I'll never understand how to use punctuation!
comma	joining two independent clauses (always with a coordinating conjunction)	Commas can be used to join independent clauses, but they must always be followed by a coordinating conjunction in order to avoid a comma splice.
	setting apart introductory and nonessential words and phrases	Commas, when used properly, set apart extra information in a sentence.
	separating three or more items in a list	My favorite punctuation marks include the colon, semicolon, and period.
semicolon	joining together two independent clauses (never with a conjunction)	I love semicolons; they make sentences so concise!
colon	introducing a list, explanation, or definition	When I see a colon I know what to expect: more information.
apostrophe	form contractions	It's amazing how many people can't use apostrophes correctly.
	show possession	The students' grammar books are out of date, but the school's principal cannot order new ones yet.
quotation marks	indicate a direct quote	I said to her, "Tell me more about parentheses."

EXAMPLES

Wrong: *Her roommate asked her to pick up milk, and a watermelon from the grocery store.*

Correct: *Her roommate asked her to pick up milk and a watermelon from the grocery store.*

Commas are only needed when joining three items in a series; this sentence only has two (milk and watermelon).

Wrong: *The softball coach—who had been in the job for only a year, quit unexpectedly on Friday.*

Correct: *The softball coach—who had been in the job for only a year—quit unexpectedly on Friday.*

Correct: *The softball coach, who had been in the job for only a year, quit unexpectedly on Friday.*

When setting apart nonessential words and phrases, **you can use either dashes or commas, but not both.**

Wrong: *I'd like to order a hamburger, with extra cheese, but my friend says I should get a fruit salad instead.*

Correct: *I'd like to order a hamburger with extra cheese, but my friend says I should get a fruit salad instead.*

Prepositional phrases are usually essential to the meaning of the sentence, so they don't need to be set apart with commas. Here, the prepositional phrase *with extra cheese* helps the reader understand that the speaker wants a particularly unhealthy meal; however, the friend is encouraging a healthier option. Removing the prepositional phrase would limit the contrast between the burger and the salad. Note that the second comma remains because it is separating two independent clauses.

Point of View

A sentence's **POINT OF VIEW** is the perspective from which it is written. Point of view is described as either first, second, or third person.

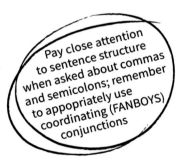

Pay close attention to sentence structure when asked about commas and semicolons; remember to appropriately use coordinating (FANBOYS) conjunctions

Table 1.4. Point of View

PERSON	PRONOUNS	WHO'S ACTING?	EXAMPLE
first	I, we	the writer	I take my time when shopping for shoes.
second	you	the reader	You prefer to shop online.
third	he, she, it, they	the subject	She buys shoes from her cousin's store.

First person perspective appears when the writer's personal experiences, feelings, and opinions are an important element of the text. Second person perspective is used when the author directly addresses the reader. Third person perspective is most common in formal and academic writing; it creates distance between the writer and the reader. A sentence's point of view must remain consistent.

 EXAMPLES

Wrong: *If someone wants to be a professional athlete, you have to practice often.*

Correct: *If you want to be a professional athlete, you have to practice often.*

Correct: *If someone wants to be a professional athlete, he or she has to practice often.*

In the first sentence, the person shifts from third (*someone*) to second (*you*). It needs to be rewritten to be consistent.

Active and Passive Voice

Sentences can be written in active voice or passive voice. **ACTIVE VOICE** means that the subjects of the sentences are performing the action of the sentence. In a sentence written in **PASSIVE VOICE**, the subjects are being acted on. The sentence *Justin wrecked my car* is in the active voice because the subject (*Justin*) is doing the action (*wrecked*). The sentence can be rewritten in passive voice by using a to be verb: *My car was wrecked by Justin*. Now the subject of the sentence (*car*) is being acted on. It's also possible to write the sentence so that the person performing the action is not identified: *My car was wrecked*.

Generally, good writing will avoid using passive voice. However, when it is unclear who or what performed the action of the sentence, passive voice may be the only option.

 EXAMPLES

Rewrite the following sentence in active voice: *I was hit with a stick by my brother.*

First, identify the person or object performing the action (usually given in a prepositional phrase—here, *by my brother*) and make it the subject; the subject of the original sentence (*I*) becomes the object. Remove the *to be* verb: **My brother hit me with a stick.**

Rewrite the following sentence in passive voice: *My roommate made coffee this morning.*

Here, the object (*coffee*) becomes the subject; move the original subject (*my roommate*) to a prepositional phrase at the end of the sentence. Add the *to be* verb: **The coffee was made this morning by my roommate.**

Transitions

TRANSITIONS connect two ideas and also explain the logical relationship between them. For example, the transition *because* tells you that two things have a cause and effect relationship, while the transitional phrase *on the other hand* introduces a contradictory idea. On the ACT English section you may be asked to identify the best transition for a particular sentence, and you will definitely need to make good use of transitions in your essay.

Table 1.5. Common Transitions

CAUSE AND EFFECT	as a result, because, consequently, due to, if/then, so, therefore, thus
SIMILARITY	also, likewise, between
CONTRAST	but, however, in contrast, on the other hand, nevertheless, on the contrary, yet
CONCLUDING	briefly, finally, in conclusion, in summary, to conclude
ADDITION	additionally, also, as well, further, furthermore, in addition, moreover
EXAMPLES	in other words, for example, for instance, to illustrate
TIME	after, before, currently, later, recently, since, subsequently, then, while

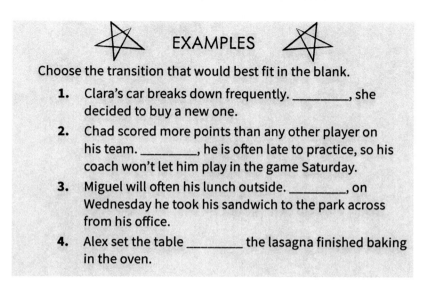

EXAMPLES

Choose the transition that would best fit in the blank.

1. Clara's car breaks down frequently. _____, she decided to buy a new one.
2. Chad scored more points than any other player on his team. _____, he is often late to practice, so his coach won't let him play in the game Saturday.
3. Miguel will often his lunch outside. _____, on Wednesday he took his sandwich to the park across from his office.
4. Alex set the table _____ the lasagna finished baking in the oven.

A) however

B) for example

C) while

D) therefore

Sentence 1 is describing a cause (*her car breaks down*) and an effect (*she'll buy a new one*), so the correct transition is *therefore*. Sentence 2 includes a contrast: it would make sense for Chad to play in the game, but he isn't, so the best transition is *however*. In Sentence 3, the clause after the transition is an example, so the best transition is *for example*. In Sentence 4, two things are occurring at the same time, so the best transition is *while*.

Wordiness and Redundancy

Sometimes sentences can be grammatically correct but still be confusing or poorly written. Often this problem arises when sentences are wordy or contain redundant phrasing (i.e., when several words with similar meanings are used). Often such phrases are used to make the writing seem more serious or academic when actually they can confuse the reader. On the test, you might be asked to clarify or even remove such phrases.

Some examples of excessive wordiness and redundancy include:

- I'll meet you in the *place where I parked my car.* → I'll meet you in the *parking lot.*
- *The point I am trying to make is that* the study was flawed.
  → The study was flawed.
- A memo was sent out *concerning the matter of* dishes left in the sink.→ A memo was sent out *about* dishes left in the sink.
- The email was *brief and to the point.* → The email was *terse.*
- I don't think I'll ever understand or comprehend Italian operas. → I don't think I'll ever understand Italian operas.

 EXAMPLES

Rewrite each of the following sentences to eliminate wordiness and redundancy.

1. The game was canceled due to the fact that a bad storm was predicted.
   → The game was canceled because a bad storm was predicted.

Replace the long phrase *due to the fact that* with the much shorter *because*.

2. The possibility exists that we will have a party for my mother's birthday.

   → We might have a party for my mother's birthday.

   By rearranging the sentence, we can replace the phrase *the possibility exists that* with the word *might*.

3. With the exception of our new puppy, all of our dogs have received their vaccinations.

   → All of our dogs have been vaccinated except our new puppy.

   The sentence can be rearranged to replace *with the exception of* with *except*. The phrase *receive their vaccinations* has also been shortened to *been vaccinated*.

4. We threw away the broken microwave that didn't work.

   → We threw away the broken microwave.

   If something is broken that means it doesn't work, so the phrase *that didn't work* can be removed.

5. It was an unexpected surprise when we won the raffle.

   → It was a surprise when we won the raffle.

   By definition, a surprise is always unexpected, so the word *unexpected* can be removed.

GO ON

Practice Questions

The Brat Pack

Anyone who has been given a nickname knows that these (1)informal labels can sometimes be difficult to shake. In the 1980s, one group of young actors earned a group nickname—the Brat Pack—that would follow them for decades. While some members of the Brat Pack still went on to have successful (2)careers; others struggled to make their own names stand out against the backdrop of the group.

The members of the Brat Pack earned their fame by appearing together in a series of films made for teen and young adult audiences. (3)Though the first one of these movies

(4)were made in the early 1980s, the Brat Pack label did not appear until 1985, when New York magazine writer David Blum wrote an article about his experience socializing with some of the group members. The

1. Which of the following options is the LEAST appropriate alternative to the underlined portion?
   A. casual designations
   B. unofficial epithets
   C. improper titles
   D. unconventional tags

2. F. NO CHANGE
   G. careers, others
   H. careers, but others
   J. careers. Others

3. A. NO CHANGE
   B. The first of
   C. Because the first of
   D. Consequently, the first of

4. F. NO CHANGE
   G. was
   H. is
   J. are

article (5)is portraying these young actors as immature, unprofessional, and spoiled, and though Blum's experience with them was limited to one night with just three individuals, his label quickly caught on and tarnished the reputations of many of the other young actors who worked alongside the three. Many of these individuals struggled professionally as a result of the negative label, and most of them denied being a part of any such group.

Today, despite the initial repercussions of the unfortunate nickname, the Brat Pack label is still in use, largely because of the (6)ongoing and perpetual relevance and significance of the Brat Pack films. Most of these films are coming-of-age stories, in which one or more of the characters gains experience or learns an important lesson about adult life. (7)For example, in the most famous of these films, *The Breakfast Club*, the five main characters,

(8)whom are all from different social circles at one high school, learn to look past labels and appearances and find that they have more in common than they ever imagined.

5. **A.** NO CHANGE
   B. would portray
   C. was portraying
   D. portrayed

6. **F.** NO CHANGE
   G. perpetually ongoing
   H. never-ending, perpetual
   J. ongoing

7. At this point in the paragraph, the writer is considering adding the following statement:

   In literary criticism, novels that center on coming-of-age stories are referred to as Bildungsroman.

   Should this addition be made?

   A. Yes; it provides more information about the types of movies the Brat Pack made.
   B. Yes; it helps the reader to understand the literary trend of coming-of-age stories.
   C. No; it distracts from the main idea of the passage.
   D. No; the Brat Pack did not write novels.

8. **F.** NO CHANGE
   G. who
   H. which
   J. and

Because of the talent and the relatability of the Brat Pack members, (9)these characters and their stories continue to appeal to young people and influence popular culture in the new millennium.

(10)Thus, the Brat Pack nickname has been freed of its negative connotations by the actors who once despised and wore the label.

9. Given that all of the following options are true, which one most effectively supports the claim made in the first sentence of the previous paragraph?

   A. NO CHANGE

   B. these movies were hugely successful in appealing to all age groups.

   C. these movies drew in enormous box-office profits.

   D. these movies propelled a few of their stars into hugely successful careers.

10. F. NO CHANGE

   G. Thus, the Brat Pack label that was worn by the actors has been freed of the negative connotations it had, making it less despised.

   H. Thus, the label that was once despised by the actors, the Brat Pack, has been altogether freed of its negative connotations.

   J. Thus, the Brat Pack nickname, which was once so despised by the actors who wore the label, has been altogether freed of its negative connotations.

GO ON

English Answer Key

1.	C.	**6.**	J.
2.	G.	**7.**	C.
3.	A.	**8.**	G.
4.	G.	**9.**	A.
5.	D.	**10.**	J.

two

MATHEMATICS
60 questions ¦ 60 minutes

The Mathematics section of the ACT consists of sixty multiple choice problems covering topics such as basic operations, algebra, geometry, and statistics.

You will be allowed to use a calculator on the Mathematics section, although all problems can be worked without one. The calculator you bring cannot have a computer algebra system (which can simplify and solve equations) or a QWERTY keyboard. You also may not use the calculator on your phone or tablet.

Strategies for the Mathematics Section

Go Back to the Basics

First and foremost, practice your basic skills: sign changes, order of operations, simplifying fractions, and equation manipulation. These are the skills used most on the ACT, though they are applied in different contexts. Remember that when it comes down to it, all math problems rely on the four basic skills of addition, subtraction, multiplication, and division. All you need to figure out is the order in which they're used to solve a problem.

Don't Rely on Mental Math

Using mental math is great for eliminating answer choices, but ALWAYS WRITE DOWN YOUR WORK! This cannot be stressed enough. Use whatever paper is provided; by writing and/or drawing out the problem, you are more likely to catch any mistakes. The act of writing things down also forces you to organize your calculations, leading to an improvement in your ACT score.

The Three-Times Rule

You should read each question at least three times to ensure you're using the correct information and answering the right question:

> Step One: Read the question and write out the given information.
>
> Step Two: Read the question, set up your equation(s), and solve.
>
> Step Three: Read the question and check that your answer makes sense (is the amount too large or small? is the answer in the correct unit of measurement? etc.).

Make an Educated Guess

Eliminate those answer choices that you are relatively sure are incorrect, and then guess from the remaining choices. Educated guessing is critical to increasing your score.

Avoid Common Mistakes

Working the math problems on the ACT requires focus and attention to detail. Don't lose points to simple mistakes such as:

- using with the wrong sign
- forgetting the order of operations
- misplacing the decimal
- answering the wrong question

Working with Positive and Negative Numbers

Adding, multiplying, and dividing numbers can yield positive or negative values depending on the signs of the original numbers. Knowing these rules can help determine if your answer is correct.

> (+) + (−) = the sign of the larger number
>
> (−) + (−) = negative number
>
> (−) × (−) = positive number
>
> (−) × (+) = negative number
>
> (−) ÷ (−) = positive number
>
> (−) ÷ (+) = negative number

EXAMPLES

Find the product of −10 and 47.

(−) × (+) = (−)

−10 × 47 = **−470**

What is the sum of −65 and −32?

(−) + (−) = (−)

−65 + −32 = **−97**

Is the product of −7 and 4 less than −7, between −7 and 4, or greater than 4?

(−) × (+) = (−)

−7 × 4 = −28, which is **less than −7**

What is the value of −16 divided by 2.5?

(−) ÷ (+) = (−)

−16 ÷ 2.5 = **−6.4**

Order of Operations

Operations in a mathematical expression are always performed in a specific order, which is described by the acronym PEMDAS:

1. Parentheses
2. Exponents
3. Multiplication
4. Division
5. Addition
6. Subtraction

Perform the operations within parentheses first, and then address any exponents. After those steps, perform all multiplication and division. These are carried out from left to right as they appear in the problem. Finally, do all required addition and subtraction, also from left to right as each operation appears in the problem.

 EXAMPLES

Solve $[-(2)^2 - (4 + 7)]$

First, complete operations within parentheses:

$-(2)^2 - (11)$

Second, calculate the value of exponential numbers:

$-(4) - (11)$

Finally, do addition and subtraction:

$-4 - 11 = \mathbf{-15}$

Solve $(5)^2 \div 5 + 4 \times 2$

First, calculate the value of exponential numbers:

$(25) \div 5 + 4 \times 2$

Second, calculate division and multiplication from left to right:

$5 + 8$

Finally, do addition and subtraction:

$5 + 8 = \mathbf{13}$

Solve the expression $15 \times (4 + 8) - 3^3$

First, complete operations within parentheses:

$15 \times (12) - 3^3$

Second, calculate the value of exponential numbers:

$15 \times (12) - 27$

Third, calculate division and multiplication from left to right:

$180 - 27$

Finally, do addition and subtraction from left to right:

$180 - 27 = \mathbf{153}$

Solve the expression $\left(\frac{5}{2} \times 4\right) + 23 - 4^2$

First, complete operations within parentheses:

$(10) + 23 - 4^2$

Second, calculate the value of exponential numbers:

$(10) + 23 - 16$

Finally, do addition and subtraction from left to right:

$(10) + 23 - 16$

$33 - 16 = \mathbf{17}$

Units of Measurement

You are expected to memorize some units of measurement. These are given below. When doing unit conversion problems (i.e., when converting one unit to another), find the conversion factor, then apply that factor to the given measurement to find the new units.

Table 2.1. Unit Prefixes

PREFIX	SYMBOL	MULTIPLICATION FACTOR
tera	T	1,000,000,000,000
giga	G	1,000,000,000
mega	M	1,000,000

kilo	k	1,000
hecto	h	100
deca	da	10
base unit	--	--
deci	d	0.1
centi	c	0.01
milli	m	0.001
micro	µ	0.0000001
nano	n	0.0000000001
pico	p	0.0000000000001

Table 2.2. Units and Conversion Factors

DIMENSION	AMERICAN	SI
length	inch/foot/yard/mile	meter
mass	ounce/pound/ton	gram
volume	cup/pint/quart/gallon	liter
force	pound-force	newton
pressure	pound-force per square inch	pascal
work and energy	cal/British thermal unit	joule
temperature	Fahrenheit	kelvin
charge	faraday	coulomb

CONVERSION FACTORS

1 in = 2.54 cm	1 lb = 0.454 kg
1 yd = 0.914 m	1 cal = 4.19 J
1 mile = 1.61 km	1 °F = 5/9 (°F − 32)
1 gallon = 3.785 L	1 cm³ = 1 mL
1 oz = 28.35 g	1 hour = 3600 s

 EXAMPLES

A fence measures 15 ft. long. How many yards long is the fence?

> 1 yd. = 3 ft.
>
> $\frac{15}{3}$ = **5 yd.**

A pitcher can hold 24 cups. How many gallons can it hold?

> 1 gal. = 16 cups
>
> $\frac{24}{16}$ = **1.5 gal.**

A spool of wire holds 144 in. of wire. If Mario has 3 spools, how many feet of wire does he have?

> 12 in. = 1 ft.

$\frac{144}{12} = 12$ ft.

12 ft. × 3 spools = **36 ft. of wire**

A ball rolling across a table travels 6 inches per second. How many feet will it travel in 1 minute?

This problem can be worked in two steps: finding how many inches are covered in 1 minute and then converting that value to feet. It can also be worked the opposite way, by finding how many feet it travels in 1 second and then converting that to feet traveled per minute. The first method is shown below.

1 min. = 60 sec.

$\frac{6 \text{ in.}}{\text{sec.}} \times 60 \text{ s} = 360$ in.

1 ft. = 12 in.

$\frac{360 \text{ in.}}{12 \text{ in.}} = $ **30 ft.**

How many millimeters are in 0.5 meters?

1 meter = 1000 mm

0.5 meters = **500 mm**

A lead ball weighs 38 g. How many kilograms does it weigh?

1 kg = 1000 g

$\frac{38 \text{ g}}{1000 \text{ g}} = $ **0.038 kg**

How many cubic centimeters are in 10 L?

1 L = 1000 cm³

10 L = 1000 cm³ × 10

10 L = **10,000 cm³**

Jennifer's pencil was initially 10 centimeters long. After she sharpened it, it was 9.6 centimeters long. How many millimeters did she lose from her pencil by sharpening it?

1 cm = 10 mm

10 cm – 9.6 cm = 0.4 cm lost

0.4 cm = 10 mm × 0.4 = **4 mm were lost**

Ratios

A ratio describes the quantity of one thing in relation to the quantity of another. Unlike fractions, ratios do not give a part relative to a whole; instead, they compare two values. For example, if you have 3 apples and 4 oranges, the ratio of apples to oranges is 3 to 4. Ratios can be written using words (3 to 4), fractions $\left(\frac{3}{4}\right)$, or colons (3:4).

It's helpful to rewrite a ratio as a fraction expressing a part to a whole. For instance, in the example above you have 7 total pieces of fruit, so the fraction of your fruit that is apples is $\frac{3}{7}$, while oranges make up $\frac{4}{7}$ of your fruit collection.

When working with ratios, always consider the units of the values being compared. On the ACT, you may be asked to rewrite a ratio using the same units on both sides. For example, you might have to rewrite the ratio 3 minutes to 7 seconds as 180 seconds to 7 seconds.

 EXAMPLES

There are 90 voters in a room, and each is either a Democrat or a Republican. The ratio of Democrats to Republicans is 5:4. How many Republicans are there?

We know that there are 5 Democrats for every 4 Republicans in the room, which means for every 9 people, 4 are Republicans.

$5 + 4 = 9$

Fraction of Democrats: $\frac{5}{9}$

Fraction of Republicans: $\frac{4}{9}$

If $\frac{4}{9}$ of the 90 voters are Republicans, then:

$\frac{4}{9} \times 90 =$ **40 voters are Republicans**

The ratio of students to teachers in a school is 15:1. If there are 38 teachers, how many students attend the school?

To solve this ratio problem, we can simply multiply both sides of the ratio by the desired value to find the number of students that correspond to having 38 teachers:

$\frac{15 \text{ students}}{1 \text{ teacher}} \times 38 \text{ teachers} = 570 \text{ students}$

The school has **570 students.**

Proportions

A proportion is an equation that equates two ratios. Proportions are usually written as two fractions joined by an equal sign $\left(\frac{a}{b} = \frac{c}{d}\right)$, but they can also be written using colons (a:b::c:d). Note that in a proportion, the units must be the same in both numerators and in both denominators.

Often you will be given three of the values in a proportion and asked to find the fourth. In these types of problems, you can solve for the missing variable by cross-multiplying—multiply the numerator of each fraction by the denominator of the other to get an equation with no fractions as shown below. You can then solve the equation using basic algebra. (For more on solving basic equations, see *Algebraic Expressions and Equations*.)

$$\frac{a}{b} = \frac{c}{d} \rightarrow ad = bc$$

 EXAMPLES

A train traveling 120 miles takes 3 hours to get to its destination. How long will it take for the train to travel 180 miles?

Start by setting up the proportion:

$$\frac{120 \text{ mi}}{3 \text{ hrs}} = \frac{180 \text{ mi}}{x \text{ hr}}$$

Note that it doesn't matter which value is placed in the numerator or denominator, as long as it is the same on both sides. Now, solve for the missing quantity through cross-multiplication:

120 mi × x hr = 3 hrs × 180 mi

Now solve the equation:

$$x \text{ hours} = \frac{3 \text{ hrs} \times 180 \text{ mi}}{120 \text{ mi}}$$

x = **4.5 hrs**

One acre of wheat requires 500 gallons of water. How many acres can be watered with 2600 gallons?

Set up the equation:

$$\frac{1 \text{ acre}}{500 \text{ gal}} = \frac{x \text{ acres}}{2600 \text{ gal}}$$

Then solve for x:

$$x \text{ acres} = \frac{1 \text{ acre} \times 2600 \text{ gal}}{500 \text{ gal}}$$

$x = \frac{26}{5}$ acres or **5.2 acres**

If 35:5::49:x, find x.

This problem presents two equivalent ratios that can be set up in a fraction equation:

$$\frac{35}{5} = \frac{49}{x}$$

You can then cross-multiply to solve for x:

35x = 49 × 5

x = **7**

Percentages

A percent is the ratio of a part to the whole. Questions may give the part and the whole and ask for the percent, or give the percent and the whole and ask for the part, or give the part and the percent and ask for the value of the whole. The equation for percentages can be rearranged to solve for any of these:

$$percent = \frac{part}{whole}$$

$$part = whole \times percent$$

$$whole = \frac{part}{percent}$$

In the equations above, the percent should always be expressed as a decimal. In order to convert a decimal into a percentage value, simply multiply it by 100. So, if you've read 5 pages (the part) of a 10-page article (the whole), you've read $\frac{5}{10}$ = .50 or 50%. (The percent sign (%) is used once the decimal has been multiplied by 100.)

Note that when solving these problems, the units for the part and the whole should be the same. If you're reading a book, saying you've read 5 pages out of 15 chapters doesn't make any sense.

> The word *of* usually indicates what the whole is in a problem. For example, the problem might say *Ella ate 2 slices of the pizza*, which means the pizza is the whole.

 EXAMPLES

45 is 15% of what number?

Set up the appropriate equation and solve. Don't forget to change 15% to a decimal value:

$$whole = \frac{part}{percent} = \frac{45}{0.15} = \textbf{300}$$

Jim spent 30% of his paycheck at the fair. He spent $15 for a hat, $30 for a shirt, and $20 playing games. How much was his check? (Round to nearest dollar.)

Set up the appropriate equation and solve:

$$whole = \frac{part}{percent} = \frac{15 + 30 + 20}{.30} = \textbf{\$217.00}$$

What percent of 65 is 39?

Set up the equation and solve:

$$percent = \frac{part}{whole} = \frac{39}{65} = \textbf{0.6 or 60\%}$$

Greta and Max sell cable subscriptions. In a given month, Greta sells 45 subscriptions and Max sells 51. If 240 total subscriptions were sold in that month, what percent were not sold by Greta or Max?

You can use the information in the question to figure out what percentage of subscriptions were sold by Max and Greta:

$$percent = \frac{part}{whole} = \frac{51 + 45}{240} = \frac{96}{240} = 0.4 \text{ or } 40\%$$

However, the question asks how many subscriptions weren't sold by Max or Greta. If they sold 40%, then the other salespeople sold 100% − 40% = **60%**.

Grant needs to score 75% on an exam. If the exam has 45 questions, at least how many does he need to answer correctly to get this score?

Set up the equation and solve. Remember to convert 75% to a decimal value:

part = whole × percent = 45 × 0.75 = 33.75, so **he needs to answer at least 34 questions correctly.**

Percent Change

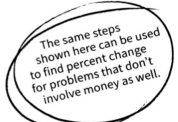

Words that indicate a percent change problem:
• Discount
• Markup
• Sale
• Increase
• Decrease

Percent change problems ask you to calculate how much a given quantity has changed. The problems are solved in a similar way to regular percent problems, except that instead of using the *part* you'll use the *amount of change*. Note that the sign of the *amount of change* is important: if the original amount has increased the change will be positive; if it has decreased the change will be negative. Again, in the equations below the percent is a decimal value; you need to multiply by 100 to get the actual percentage.

$$percent\ change = \frac{amount\ of\ change}{original\ amount}$$

$$amount\ of\ change = original\ amount \times percent\ change$$

$$original\ amount = \frac{amount\ of\ change}{percent\ change}$$

The same steps shown here can be used to find percent change for problems that don't involve money as well.

 EXAMPLES

A computer software retailer marks up its games by 40% above the wholesale price when it sells them to customers. Find the price of a game for a customer if the game costs the retailer $25.

Set up the appropriate equation and solve:

amount of change = original amount × percent change →

25 × 0.4 = 10

If the amount of change is 10, that means the store adds a markup of $10, so the game costs:

$25 + $10 = **$35**

A golf shop pays its wholesaler $40 for a certain club, and then sells it to a golfer for $75. What is the markup rate?

First, calculate the amount of change:

75 − 40 = 35

Now you can set up the equation and solve. (Note that markup rate is another way of saying percent change):

$$percent\ change = \frac{amount\ of\ change}{original\ amount} \rightarrow$$

$\frac{35}{40}$ = 0.875 = **87.5%**

A shoe store charges a 40% markup on the shoes it sells. How much did the store pay for a pair of shoes purchased by a customer for $63?

You're solving for the original price, but it's going to be tricky because you don't know the amount of change; you only know the new price. To solve, you need to create an expression for the amount of change:

If original amount = x

Then amount of change = $63 - x$

Now you can plug these values into your equation:

$$original\ amount = \frac{amount\ of\ change}{percent\ change}$$

$$x = \frac{63 - x}{0.4}$$

The last step is to solve for x:

$0.4x = 63 - x$

$1.4x = 63$

$x = 45 \rightarrow$ **The store paid $45 for the shoes.**

An item originally priced at $55 is marked 25% off. What is the sale price?

You've been asked to find the sale price, which means you need to solve for the amount of change first:

amount of change = original amount × percent change = 55 × 0.25 = 13.75

Using this amount, you can find the new price. Because it's on sale, we know the item will cost less than the original price:

55 − 13.75 = 41.25

The sale price is **$41.25**.

James wants to put an 18 foot by 51 foot garden in his backyard. If he does, it will reduce the size of his yard by 24%. What will be the area of the remaining yard space?

This problem is tricky because you need to figure out what each number in the problem stands for. 24% is obviously the percent change, but what about the measurements in feet? If you multiply these values you get the area of the garden (for more on area see *Area and Perimeter*):

18 ft. × 51 ft. = 918 ft.²

This 918 ft.² is the amount of change—it's how much area the yard lost to create the garden. Now you can set up an equation:

$$original\ amount = \frac{amount\ of\ change}{percent\ change} = \frac{918}{.24} = 3825$$

If the original lawn was 3825 ft.² and the garden is 918 ft.², then the remaining area is:

$$3825 - 918 = 2907$$

The remaining lawn covers 2907 ft.²

Comparison of Rational Numbers

Number comparison problems present numbers in different formats and ask which is larger or smaller, or whether the numbers are equivalent. The important step in solving these problems is to convert the numbers to the same format so that it is easier to compare them. If numbers are given in the same format, or after converting them, determine which number is smaller or if the numbers are equal. Remember that for negative numbers, higher numbers are actually smaller.

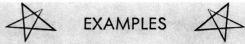 EXAMPLES

Is $4\frac{3}{4}$ greater than, equal to, or less than $\frac{18}{4}$?

These numbers are in different formats—one is a mixed fraction and the other is just a fraction. So, the first step is to convert the mixed fraction to a fraction:

$$4\frac{3}{4} = 4 \times \frac{4}{4} + \frac{3}{4} = \frac{19}{4}$$

Once the mixed number is converted, it is easier to see that $\frac{19}{4}$ **is greater than** $\frac{18}{4}$.

Which of the following numbers has the greatest value: 104.56, 104.5, or 104.6?

These numbers are already in the same format, so the decimal values just need to be compared. Remember that zeros can be added after the decimal without changing the value, so the three numbers can be rewritten as:

104.56

104.50

104.60

From this list, it is clearer that **104.60 is the greatest** because 0.60 is larger than 0.50 and 0.56.

Is 65% greater than, less than, or equal to $\frac{13}{20}$?

The first step is to convert the numbers into the same format—65% is the same as $\frac{65}{100}$.

Next, the fractions need to be converted to have the same denominator because it is difficult to compare fractions with different denominators. Using a factor of $\frac{5}{5}$ on the second fraction will give common denominators: $\frac{13}{20} \times \frac{5}{5} = \frac{65}{100}$. Now it is easy to see that **the numbers are equivalent.**

Exponents and Radicals

Exponents tell us how many times to multiply a base number by itself. In the example 2^4, 2 is the base number and 4 is the exponent. $2^4 = 2 \times 2 \times 2 \times 2 = 16$. Exponents are also called powers: 5 to the third power = $5^3 = 5 \times 5 \times 5 = 125$. Some exponents have special names: x to the second power is also called "x squared" and x to the third power is also called "x cubed." The number 3 squared = $3^2 = 3 \times 3 = 9$.

Radicals are expressions that use roots. Radicals are written in the form $\sqrt[a]{x}$ where a = the **RADICAL POWER** and x = **THE RADICAND**. The solution to the radical $\sqrt[3]{8}$ is the number that, when multiplied by itself 3 times, equals 8. $\sqrt[3]{8} = 2$ because $2 \times 2 \times 2 = 8$. When the radical power is not written we assume it is 2, so $\sqrt{9} = 3$ because $3 \times 3 = 9$. Radicals can also be written as exponents, where the power is a fraction. For example, $x^{\frac{1}{3}} = \sqrt[3]{x}$.

Review more of the rules for working with exponents and radicals in the table below.

Table 2.3. Exponents and Radicals Rules

RULE	EXAMPLE
$x^0 = 1$	$5^0 = 1$
$x^1 = x$	$5^1 = 5$
$x^a \times x^b = x^{a+b}$	$5^2 \times 5^3 = 5^5 = 3125$
$(xy)^a = x^a y^a$	$(5 \times 6)^2 = 5^2 \times 6^2 = 900$
$(x^a)^b = x^{ab}$	$(5^2)^3 = 5^6 = 15{,}625$
$\left(\frac{x}{y}\right)^a = \frac{x^a}{y^b}$	$\left(\frac{5}{6}\right)^2 = \frac{5^2}{6^2} = \frac{25}{36}$
$\frac{x^a}{x^b} = x^{a-b} \ (x \neq 0)$	$\frac{5^4}{5^3} = 5^1 = 5$

$$x^{-a} = \frac{1}{x^a} \; (x \neq 0) \qquad\qquad 5^{-2} = \frac{1}{5^2} = \frac{1}{25}$$

$$x^{\frac{1}{a}} = \sqrt[a]{x} \qquad\qquad 25^{\frac{1}{2}} = \sqrt[2]{25} = 5$$

$$\sqrt[a]{x \times y} = \sqrt[a]{x} \times \sqrt[a]{y} \qquad \sqrt[3]{8 \times 27} = \sqrt[3]{8} \times \sqrt[3]{27} = 2 \times 3 = 6$$

$$\sqrt[a]{\frac{x}{y}} = \frac{\sqrt[a]{x}}{\sqrt[a]{y}} \qquad\qquad \sqrt[3]{\frac{27}{8}} = \frac{\sqrt[3]{27}}{\sqrt[3]{8}} = \frac{3}{2}$$

$$\sqrt[a]{x^b} = x^{\frac{b}{a}} \qquad\qquad \sqrt[2]{5^4} = 5^{\frac{4}{2}} = 5^2 = 25$$

 EXAMPLES

Simplify the expression $2^4 \times 2^2$

When multiplying exponents in which the base number is the same, simply add the powers:

$2^4 \times 2^2 = 2^{(4+2)} = 2^6$

$2^6 = 2 \times 2 \times 2 \times 2 \times 2 \times 2 = \textbf{64}$

Simplify the expression $(3^4)^{-1}$

When an exponent is raised to a power, multiply the powers:

$(3^4)^{-1} = 3^{-4}$

When the exponent is a negative number, rewrite as the reciprocal of the positive exponent:

$3^{-4} = \frac{1}{3^4}$

$\frac{1}{3^4} = \frac{1}{3 \times 3 \times 3 \times 3} = \frac{1}{\textbf{81}}$

Simplify the expression $\left(\frac{9}{4}\right)^{\frac{1}{2}}$

When the power is a fraction, rewrite as a radical:

$\left(\frac{9}{4}\right)^{\frac{1}{2}} = \sqrt{\frac{9}{4}}$

Next, distribute the radical to the numerator and denominator:

$\sqrt{\frac{9}{4}} = \frac{\sqrt{9}}{\sqrt{4}} = \frac{\textbf{3}}{\textbf{2}}$

Algebraic Expressions

Algebraic expressions and equations include VARIABLES, or letters standing in for numbers. These expressions and equations are made up of terms, which are groups of numbers and variables (e.g., $2xy$). An expression is simply a set of terms (e.g., $\frac{2x}{3yz} + 2$). When those terms are joined only by addition or subtraction, the expression is called a **POLYNOMIAL** (e.g., $2x + 3yz$). When working with expressions, you'll need to use many different mathematical properties and operations, including addition/subtraction, multiplication/division, exponents, roots, distribution, and the order of operations.

Evaluating Algebraic Expressions

To evaluate an algebraic expression, simply plug the given value(s) in for the appropriate variable(s) in the expression.

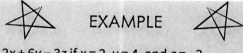 EXAMPLE

Evaluate $2x + 6y - 3z$ if $x = 2$, $y = 4$, and $z = -3$.

Plug in each number for the correct variable and simplify:
$2x + 6y - 3z = 2(2) + 6(4) - 3(-3) = 4 + 24 + 9 = \mathbf{37}$

Adding and Subtracting Expressions

Only **LIKE TERMS**, which have the exact same variable(s), can be added or subtracted. **CONSTANTS** are numbers without variables attached, and those can be added and subtracted together as well. When simplifying an expression, like terms should be added or subtracted so that no individual group of variables occurs in more than one term. For example, the expression $5x + 6xy$ is in its simplest form, while $5x + 6xy - 11xy$ is not because the term xy appears more than once.

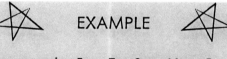 EXAMPLE

Simplify the expression $5xy + 7y + 2yz + 11xy - 5yz$

Start by grouping together like terms:
$(5xy + 11xy) + (2yz - 5yz) + 7y$
Now you can add together each set of like terms:
$\mathbf{16xy + 7y - 3yz}$

Multiplying and Dividing Expressions

To multiply a single term by another, simply multiply the coefficients and then multiply the variables. Remember that when multiplying variables with exponents, those exponents are added together. For example: $(x^5 y)(x^3 y^4) = x^8 y^5$.

When multiplying a term by a set of terms inside parentheses, you need to distribute to each term inside the parentheses as follows:

$$\mathbf{a(b + c) = ab + ac}$$

Figure 2.1. Distribution

When variables occur in both the numerator and denominator of a fraction, they cancel each other out. So, a fraction with variables in its simplest form will not have the same variable on the top and bottom.

 EXAMPLES

Simplify the expression $(3x^4 y^2z)(2y^4z^5)$.

Multiply the coefficients and variables together:

$3 \times 2 = 6$

$y^2 \times y^4 = y^6$

$z \times z^5 = z^6$

Now put all the terms back together:

$6x^4y^6z^6$

Simplify the expression: $(2y^2)(y^3 + 2xy^2z + 4z)$

Multiply each term inside the parentheses by the term $2y^2$:

$(2y^2)(y^3 + 2xy^2z + 4z) =$

$(2y^2 \times y^3) + (2y^2 \times 2xy^2z) \times (2y^2 \times 4z) =$

$2y^5 + 4xy^4z + 8y^2z$

Simplify the expression: $(5x + 2)(3x + 3)$

Use the acronym FOIL—first, outer, inner, last—to multiply the terms:

first: $5x \times 3x = 15x^2$

outer: $5x \times 3 = 15x$

inner: $2 \times 3x = 6x$

last: $2 \times 3 = 6$

Now combine like terms:

$15x^2 + 21x + 6$

Simplify the expression: $\frac{2x^4y^3z}{8x^2z^2}$

Simplify by looking at each variable and checking for those that appear in the numerator and denominator:

$\frac{2}{8} = \frac{1}{4}$

$\frac{x^4}{x^2} = \frac{x^2}{1}$

$\frac{z}{z^2} = \frac{1}{z}$

$\frac{2x^4y^3z}{8x^2z^2} = \frac{x^2y^3}{4z}$

Factoring Expressions

Factoring is splitting one expression into the multiplication of two expressions. It requires finding the highest common factor and dividing terms by that number. For example, in the expression $15x + 10$, the highest common factor is 5 because both terms are divisible by 5: $\frac{15x}{5} = 3x$ and $\frac{10}{5} = 2$. When you factor the expression you get $5(3x + 2)$.

Sometimes it is difficult to find the highest common factor. In these cases, consider whether the expression fits a polynomial identity. A polynomial is an expression with more than one term. If you can recognize the common polynomials listed below, you can easily factor the expression.

$a^2 - b^2 = (a + b)(a - b)$

$a^2 + 2ab + b^2 = (a + b)(a + b) = (a + b)^2$

$a^2 - 2ab + b^2 = (a - b)(a - b) = (a - b)^2$

$a^3 + b^3 = (a + b)(a^2 - ab + b^2)$

$a^3 - b^3 = (a - b)(a^2 + ab + b^2)$

 EXAMPLES

Factor the expression $25x^2 - 16$

Since there is no obvious factor by which you can divide terms, you should consider whether this expression fits one of your polynomial identities.

This expression is a difference of squares: $a^2 - b^2$, where $a^2 = 25x^2$ and $b^2 = 16$.

Recall that $a^2 - b^2 = (a + b)(a - b)$. Now solve for a and b:

$a = 25x^2 = 5x$

$b = \sqrt{16} = 4$

$(a + b)(a - b) = $ **$(5x + 4)(5x - 4)$**

You can check your work by using the FOIL acronym to expand your answer back to the original expression:

first: $5x \times 5x = 25x^2$

outer: $5x \times -4 = -20x$

inner: $4 \times 5x = 20x$

last: $4 \times -4 = -16$

$25x^2 - 20x + 20x - 16 = 25x^2 - 16$

Factor the expression $27x^2 - 9x$

First, find the highest common factor. Both terms are divisible by 9:

$\frac{27x^2}{9} = 3x^2$ and $\frac{9x}{9} = x$

Now the expression is $9(3x^2 - x)$—but wait, you're not done! Both terms can be divided by x:

$\frac{3x^2}{x} = 3x$ and $\frac{x}{x} = 1$.

The final factored expression is **$9x(3x - 1)$**.

Factor the expression $100x^2 + 60x + 9$

This is another polynomial identity, $a^2 + 2ab + b^2$. (The more you practice these problems, the faster you will recognize polynomial identities.)

$a^2 = 100x^2$, $2ab = 60x$, and $b^2 = 9$

Recall that $a^2 + 2ab + b^2 = (a + b)^2$. Now solve for a and b:

$a = \sqrt{100x^2} = 10x$

$b = \sqrt{9} = 3$

(Double check your work by confirming that $2ab = 2 \times 10x \times 3 = 60x$)

$(a + b)^2 = \mathbf{(10x + 3)^2}$

Linear Equations

An **EQUATION** is a statement saying that two expressions are equal to each other. They always include an equal sign (e.g., $3x + 2xy = 17$). A **LINEAR EQUATION** has only two variables; on a graph, linear equations form a straight line.

Solving Linear Equations

To solve an equation, you need to manipulate the terms on each side to isolate the variable, meaning if you want to find x, you have to get the x alone on one side of the equal sign. To do this, you'll need to use many of the tools discussed above: you might need to distribute, divide, add, or subtract like terms, or find common denominators.

Think of each side of the equation as the two sides of a see-saw. As long as the two people on each end weigh the same amount (no matter what it is) the see-saw will be balanced: if you have a 120 pound person on each end, the see-saw is balanced. Giving each of them a 10 pound rock to hold changes the weight on each end, but the see-saw itself stays balanced. Equations work the same way: you can add, subtract, multiply, or divide whatever you want as long as you do the same thing to both sides.

Most equations you'll see on the ACT can be solved using the same basic steps:

1. Distribute to get rid of parentheses.
2. Use LCD to get rid of fractions.
3. Add/subtract like terms on either side.
4. Add/subtract so that constants appear on only one side of the equation.
5. Multiply/divide to isolate the variable.

EXAMPLES

Solve for x: $25x + 12 = 62$

This equation has no parentheses, fractions, or like terms on the same side, so you can start by subtracting 12 from both sides of the equation:

$25x + 12 = 62$

$(25x + 12) - 12 = 62 - 12$

$25x = 50$

Now, divide by 25 to isolate the variable:

$\frac{25x}{25} = \frac{50}{25}$

$x = 2$

Solve the following equation for x: $2x - 4(2x + 3) = 24$

Start by distributing to get rid of the parentheses (don't forget to distribute the negative):

$2x - 4(2x + 3) = 24 \rightarrow$

$2x - 8x - 12 = 24$

There are no fractions, so now you can join like terms:

$2x - 8x - 12 = 24 \rightarrow$

$-6x - 12 = 24$

Now add 12 to both sides and divide by -6.

$-6x - 12 = 24 \rightarrow$

$(-6x - 12) + 12 = 24 + 12 \rightarrow$

$-6x = 36 \rightarrow$

$\frac{-6x}{-6} = \frac{36}{-6}$

$x = -6$

Solve the following equation for x: $\frac{x}{3} + \frac{1}{2} = \frac{x}{6} - \frac{5}{12}$

Start by multiplying by the least common denominator to get rid of the fractions:

$\frac{x}{3} + \frac{1}{2} = \frac{x}{6} - \frac{5}{12} \rightarrow$

$12\left(\frac{x}{3} + \frac{1}{2}\right) = 12\left(\frac{x}{6} - \frac{5}{12}\right) \rightarrow$

$4x + 6 = 2x - 5$

Now you can isolate the x:

$(4x + 6) - 6 = (2x - 5) - 6 \rightarrow$

$4x = 2x - 11 \rightarrow$

$(4x) - 2x = (2x - 11) - 2x \rightarrow$

$2x = -11$

$x = -\frac{11}{2}$

Find the value of x: $2(x + y) - 7x = 14x + 3$

> This equation looks more difficult because it has 2 variables, but you can use the same steps to solve for x. First, distribute to get rid of the parentheses and combine like terms:
>
> $2(x + y) - 7x = 14x + 3 \rightarrow$
>
> $2x + 2y - 7x = 14x + 3 \rightarrow$
>
> $-5x + 2y = 14x + 3$
>
> Now you can move the x terms to one side and everything else to the other, and then divide to isolate x:
>
> $-5x + 2y = 14x + 3 \rightarrow$
>
> $-19x = -2y + 3 \rightarrow$
>
> $x = \dfrac{2y - 3}{19}$

Graphing Linear Equations

Linear equations can be plotted as straight lines on a coordinate plane. The X-AXIS is always the horizontal axis and the Y-AXIS is always the vertical axis. The x-axis is positive to the right of the y-axis and negative to the left. The y-axis is positive above the x-axis and negative below. To describe the location of any point on the graph, write the coordinates in the form (x, y). The origin, the point where the x- and y-axes cross, is $(0, 0)$.

The Y-INTERCEPT is the y coordinate where the line crosses the y-axis. The SLOPE is a measure of how steep the line is. Slope is calculated by dividing the change along the y-axis by the change along the x-axis between any two points on the line.

Linear equations are easiest to graph when they are written in POINT-SLOPE FORM: $y = mx + b$. The constant m represents slope and the constant b represents the y-intercept. If you know two points along the line (x_1, y_1) and (x_2, y_2), you can calculate slope using the following equation: $m = \dfrac{y_2 - y_1}{x_2 - x_1}$. If you know the slope and one other point along the line, you can calculate the y-intercept by plugging the number 0 in for x_2 and solving for y_2.

When graphing a linear equation, first plot the y-intercept. Next, plug in values for x to solve for y and plot additional points. Connect the points with a straight line.

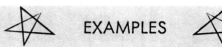 EXAMPLES

Find the slope of the line: $\dfrac{3y}{2} + 3 = x$

> Slope is easiest to find when the equation is in point-slope form: $(y = mx + b)$. Rearrange the equation to isolate y:

$$\frac{3y}{2} + 3 = x$$

$$3y + 6 = 2x$$

$$y + 2 = \frac{2x}{3}$$

$$y = \frac{2x}{3} - 2$$

Finally, identify the term m to find the slope of the line:

$$m = \frac{2}{3}$$

Plot the linear equation $2y - 4x = 6$

First, rearrange the linear equation to point-slope form
$(y = mx + b)$:

$$2y - 4x = 6$$

$$y = 2x + 3$$

Next, identify the y-intercept (b) and the slope (m):

$$b = 3, m = 2$$

Now, plot the y-intercept $(0, b) = (0, 3)$:

Next, plug in values for x and solve for y:

$$y = 2(1) + 3 = 5 \rightarrow (1, 5)$$

$$y = 2(-1) + 3 = 1 \rightarrow (-1, 1)$$

Plot these points on the graph, and connect the points with
a straight line:

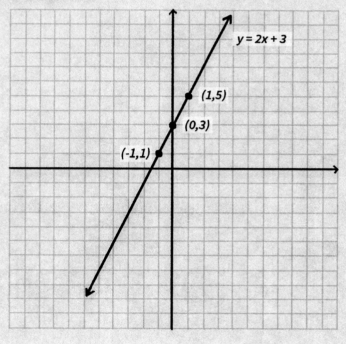

Systems of Equations

A system of equations is a group of related questions sharing the
same variable. The problems you see on the ACT will most likely
involve two equations that each have two variables, although you
may also solve sets of equations with any number of variables as long

as there are a corresponding number of equations (e.g., to solve a system with four variables, you need four equations).

There are two main methods used to solve systems of equations. In SUBSTITUTION, solve one equation for a single variable, then substitute the solution for that variable into the second equation to solve for the other variable. Or, you can use ELIMINATION by adding equations together to cancel variables and solve for one of them.

 EXAMPLES

Solve the following system of equations: $3y - 4 + x = 0$ and $5x + 6y = 11$

To solve this system using substitution, first solve one equation for a single variable:

$3y - 4 + x = 0$

$3y + x = 4$

$x = 4 - 3y$

Next, substitute the expression to the right of the equal sign for x in the second equation:

$5x + 6y = 11$

$5(4 - 3y) + 6y = 11$

$20 - 15y + 6y = 11$

$20 - 9y = 11$

$-9y = -9$

$y = 1$

Finally, plug the value for y back into the first equation to find the value of x:

$3y - 4 + x = 0$

$3(1) - 4 + x = 0$

$-1 + x = 0$

$x = 1$

The solution is $x = 1$ and $y = 1$, or the point **(1, 1)**.

Solve the system $2x + 4y = 8$ and $4x + 2y = 10$

To solve this system using elimination, start by manipulating one equation so that a variable (in this case x) will cancel when the equations are added together:

$2x + 4y = 8$

$-2(2x + 4y = 8)$

$-4x - 8y = -16$

Now you can add the two equations together, and the x variable will drop out:

$$-4x - 8y = -16$$
$$\underline{\ 4x + 2y = 10\ }$$
$$-6y = -6$$
$$y = 1$$

Lastly, plug the y value into one of the equations to find the value of x:

$$2x + 4y = 8$$
$$2x + 4(1) = 8$$
$$2x + 4 = 8$$
$$2x = 4$$
$$x = 2$$

The solution is **$x = 2$ and $y = 1$**, or the point **(2, 1)**.

Building Equations

Word problems describe a situation or a problem without explicitly providing an equation to solve. It is up to you to build an algebraic equation to solve the problem. You must translate the words into mathematical operations. Represent the quantity you do not know with a variable. If there is more than one unknown, you will likely have to write more than one equation, then solve the system of equations by substituting expressions. Make sure you keep your variables straight!

 EXAMPLES

David, Jesse, and Mark shoveled snow during their snow day and made a total of $100. They agreed to split it based on how much each person worked. David will take $10 more than Jesse, who will take $15 more than Mark. How much money will David get?

Start by building an equation. David's amount will be d, Jesse's amount will be j, and Mark's amount will be m. All three must add up to $100:

$$d + j + m = 100$$

It may seem like there are three unknowns in this situation, but you can express j and m in terms of d:

Jesse gets $10 less than David, so $j = d - 10$. Mark gets $15 less than Jesse, so $m = j - 15$.

Substitute the previous expression for j to solve for m in terms of d:

$$m = (d - 10) - 15 = d - 25$$

Now back to our original equation, substituting for j and m:

$$d + (d - 10) + (d - 25) = 100$$

$$3d - 35 = 100$$
$$3d = 135$$
$$d = 45$$

David will get **$45.**

The sum of three consecutive numbers is 54. What is the middle number?

Start by building an equation. One of the numbers in question will be x. The three numbers are consecutive, so if x is the smallest number then the other two numbers must be $(x + 1)$ and $(x + 2)$. You know that the sum of the three numbers is 54:

$$x + (x + 1) + (x + 2) = 54$$

Now solve for the equation to find x:

$$3x + 3 = 54$$
$$3x = 51$$
$$x = 17$$

The question asks about the middle number $(x + 1)$, so the answer is **18.**

Notice that you could have picked any number to be x. If you picked the middle number as x, your equation would be $(x - 1) + x + (x + 1) = 54$. Solve for x to get 18.

There are 42 people on the varsity football team. This is 8 more than half the number of people on the swim team. There are 6 fewer boys on the swim team than girls. How many girls are on the swim team?

This word problem might seem complicated at first, but as long as you keep your variables straight and translate the words into mathematical operations you can easily build an equation. The quantity you want to solve is the number of girls on the swim team, so this will be x.

The number of boys on the swim team will be y. There are 6 fewer boys than girls so $y = x - 6$.

The total number of boys and girls on the swim team is $x + y$.

42 is 8 more than half this number, so $42 = 8 + (x + y) \div 2$

Now substitute for y to solve for x:

$$42 = 8 + (x + x - 6) \div 2$$
$$34 = (2x - 6) \div 2$$
$$68 = 2x - 6$$
$$74 = 2x$$
$$x = 37$$

There are 37 girls on the swim team.

Linear Inequalities

INEQUALITIES look like equations, except that instead of having an equal sign, they have one of the following symbols:

> \> greater than: the expression left of the symbol is larger than the expression on the right

> \< less than: the expression left of the symbol is smaller than the expression on the right

> ≥ greater than or equal to: the expression left of the symbol is larger than or equal to the expression on the right

> ≤ less than or equal to: the expression left of the symbol is less than or equal to the expression on the right

Solving Linear Inequalities

Inequalities are solved like linear and algebraic equations. The only difference is that the symbol must be reversed when both sides of the equation are multiplied by a negative number.

 EXAMPLES

Solve for x: $-7x + 2 < 6 - 5x$

Collect like terms on each side as you would for a regular equation:

$-7x + 2 < 6 - 5x \rightarrow$

$-2x < 4$

When you divide by a negative number, the direction of the sign switches:

$-2x < 4 = x > -2$

Graphing Linear Inequalities

Graphing a linear inequality is just like graphing a linear equation, except that you shade the area on one side of the line. To graph a linear inequality, first rearrange the inequality expression into $y = mx + b$ form. Then treat the inequality symbol like an equal sign and plot the line. If the inequality symbol is < or >, make a broken line; for ≤ or ≥, make a solid line. Finally, shade the correct side of the graph:

For $y < mx + b$ or $y ≤ mx + b$, shade below the line.

For $y > mx + b$ or $y ≥ mx + b$, shade above the line.

GO ON

Plot the inequality $-3x \geq 4 - y$

To rearrange the inequality into $y = mx + b$ form, first subtract 4 from both sides:

$-3x - 4 \geq -y$

Next divide both sides by -1 to get positive y; remember to switch the direction of the inequality symbol:

$3x + 4 \leq y$

Now plot the line $y = 3x + 4$, making a solid line:

Finally, shade the side above the line:

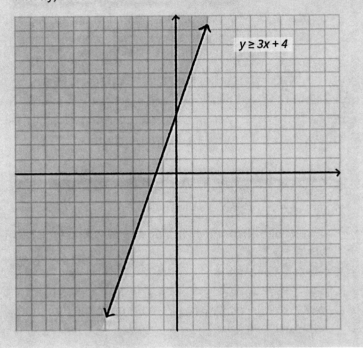

$y \geq 3x + 4$

Quadratic Equations

A quadratic equation is any equation in the form $ax^2 + bx + c = 0$. In quadratic equations, x is the variable and a, b, and c are all known numbers. a cannot be 0.

Solving Quadratic Equations

There is more than one way to solve a quadratic equation. One way is by FACTORING. By rearranging the expression $ax^2 + bx + c$ into one factor multiplied by another factor, you can easily solve for the ROOTS, the values of x for which the quadratic expression equals 0. Another way to solve a quadratic equation is by using the QUADRATIC FORMULA: $x = \frac{-b \pm \sqrt{b^2 - 4ac}}{2a}$. The expression $b^2 - 4ac$ is called the DISCRIMINANT; when it is positive you will get two real numbers for x, when it is negative you will get one real number and one imaginary number for x, and when it is zero you will get one real number for x.

 EXAMPLES

Factor the quadratic equation $-2x^2 = 14x$ and find the roots.

Not every quadratic equation you see will be presented in the standard form. Rearrange terms to set one side equal to 0:

$2x^2 + 14x = 0$

Note that $a = 2$, $b = 14$, and $c = 0$ because there is no third term.

Now divide the expression on the left by the common factor:

$(2x)(x + 7) = 0$

To find the roots, set each of the factors equal to 0:

$2x = 0 \rightarrow x = \mathbf{0}$

$x + 7 = 0 \rightarrow x = \mathbf{-7}$

Use the quadratic formula to solve for x: $3x^2 = 7x - 2$

First rearrange the equation to set one side equal to 0:

$3x^2 - 7x + 2 = 0$

Next identify the terms a, b, and c:

$a = 3$, $b = -7$, $c = 2$

Now plug those terms into the quadratic formula:

$x = \dfrac{-b \pm \sqrt{b^2 - 4ac}}{2a}$

$x = \dfrac{7 \pm \sqrt{(-7)^2 - 4(3)(2)}}{2(3)}$

$x = \dfrac{7 \pm \sqrt{25}}{6}$

$x = \dfrac{7 \pm 5}{6}$

Since the determinant is positive, you can expect two real numbers for x. Solve for the two possible answers:

$x = \dfrac{7 + 5}{6} \rightarrow x = \mathbf{2}$

$x = \dfrac{7 - 5}{6} \rightarrow x = \mathbf{\dfrac{1}{3}}$

Graphing Quadratic Equations

Graphing a quadratic equation forms a PARABOLA. A parabola is a symmetrical, horseshoe-shaped curve; a vertical axis passes through its vertex. Each term in the equation $ax^2 + bx + c = 0$ affects the shape of the parabola. A bigger value for a makes the curve narrower, while a smaller value makes the curve wider. A negative value for a flips the parabola upside down. The AXIS OF SYMMETRY is the vertical line $x = \dfrac{-b}{2a}$. To find the y-coordinate for the VERTEX (the highest or lowest point on the parabola), plug this value for x into the expression $ax^2 + bx + c$. The easiest way to graph a quadratic equation is to find the axis of symmetry, solve for the vertex, and then create a table of points by plugging in other numbers for x and solving for y. Plot these points and trace the parabola.

 EXAMPLES

Graph the equation $x^2 + 4x + 1 = 0$

First, find the axis of symmetry. The equation for the line of symmetry is $x = \frac{-b}{2a}$.

$x = \frac{-4}{2(1)} = -2$

Next, plug in −2 for x to find the y coordinate of the vertex:

$y = (-2)^2 + 4(-2) + 1 = -3$

The vertex is (−2, −3).

Now, make a table of points on either side of the vertex by plugging in numbers for x and solving for y:

x	$y = x^2 + 4x + 1$	(x, y)
−3	$y = (-3)^2 + 4(-3) + 1 = -2$	(−3, −2)
−1	$y = (-1)^2 + 4(-1) + 1 = -2$	(−1, −2)
−4	$y = (-4)^2 + 4(-4) + 1 = 1$	(−4, 1)
0	$y = 0^2 + 4(0) + 1 = 1$	(0, 1)

Finally, draw the axis of symmetry, plot the vertex and your table of points, and trace the parabola:

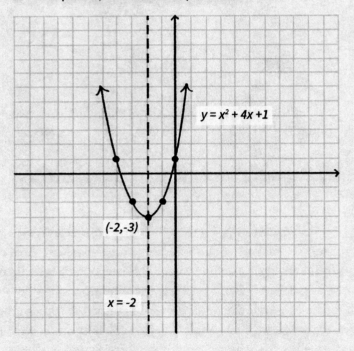

$y = x^2 + 4x + 1$

(-2,-3)

$x = -2$

Functions

FUNCTIONS describe how an input relates to an output. Linear equations, sine, and cosine are examples of functions. In a function, there must be one and only one output for each input. $\sqrt{x}$ is not a function because there are two outputs for any one input: $\sqrt{4} = 2, -2$.

Describing Functions

Functions are often written in *f(x)* form: $f(x) = x^2$ means that for input x the output is x^2. In relating functions to linear equations, you can think of $f(x)$ as equivalent to y. The DOMAIN of a function is all the possible inputs of that function. The RANGE of a function includes the outputs of the inputs. For example, for the function $f(x) = x^2$, if the domain includes all positive and negative integers the range will include 0 and only positive integers. When you graph a function, the domain is plotted on the x-axis and the range is plotted on the y-axis.

 EXAMPLES

Given $f(x) = 2x - 10$, find $f(9)$.

Plug in 9 for x:

$f(9) = 2(9) - 10$

$f(9) = 8$

Given $f(x) = \frac{4}{x}$ with a domain of all positive integers except zero, and $g(x) = \frac{4}{x}$ with a domain of all positive and negative integers except zero, which function has a range that includes the number −2?

The function $f(x)$ has a range of only positive numbers, since x cannot be negative. The function $g(x)$ has a range of positive and negative numbers, since x can be either positive or negative.

The number −2, therefore, must be in the range for $g(x)$ but not for $f(x)$.

Exponential Functions

An EXPONENTIAL FUNCTION is in the form $f(x) = a^x$, where $a > 0$. When $a > 1$, $f(x)$ approaches infinity as x increases and zero as x decreases. When $0 < a < 1$, $f(x)$ approaches zero as x increases and infinity as x increases. When $a = 1$, $f(x) = 1$. The graph of an exponential function where $a \neq 1$ will have a horizontal asymptote along the x-axis; the graph will never cross below the x-axis. The graph of an exponential function where $a = 1$ will be a horizontal line at $y = 1$. All graphs of exponential functions include the points $(0, 1)$ and $(1, a)$.

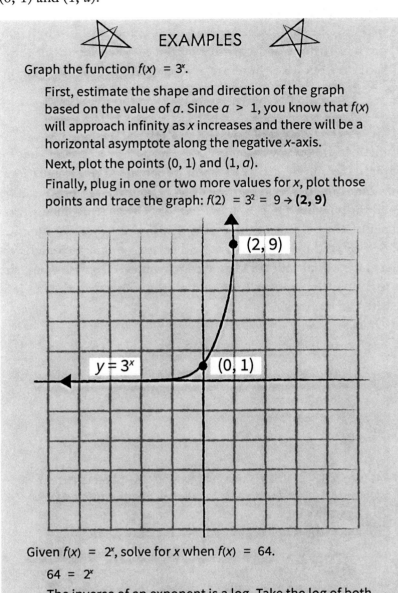

⭐ EXAMPLES ⭐

Graph the function $f(x) = 3^x$.

First, estimate the shape and direction of the graph based on the value of a. Since $a > 1$, you know that $f(x)$ will approach infinity as x increases and there will be a horizontal asymptote along the negative x-axis.

Next, plot the points $(0, 1)$ and $(1, a)$.

Finally, plug in one or two more values for x, plot those points and trace the graph: $f(2) = 3^2 = 9 \rightarrow$ **(2, 9)**

Given $f(x) = 2^x$, solve for x when $f(x) = 64$.

$64 = 2^x$

The inverse of an exponent is a log. Take the log of both sides to solve for x:

$\log_2 64 = x$

$x = 6$

Logarithmic Functions

A **LOGARITHMIC FUNCTION** is the inverse of an exponential function. Remember the definition of a log: if $\log_a x = b$, then $a^b = x$. Logarithmic functions are written in the form $f(x) = \log_a x$, where a is any number greater than 0, except for 1. If a is not shown, it is assumed that $a = 10$. The function $\ln x$ is called a **NATURAL LOG**, equal to $\log_e x$. When $0 < a < 1$, $f(x)$ approaches infinity as x approaches zero and negative infinity as x increases. When $a > 1$, $f(x)$ approaches negative infinity as x approaches zero and infinity as x

increases. In either case, the graph of a logarithmic function has a vertical asymptote along the y-axis; the graph will never cross to the left of the y-axis. All graphs of logarithmic functions include the points $(1, 0)$ and $(a, 1)$.

 EXAMPLES

Graph the function $f(x) = \log_4 x$

First, estimate the shape and direction of the graph based on the value of a. Since $a > 1$, you know that $f(x)$ will approach infinity as x increases and there will be a vertical asymptote along the negative y-axis.

Next, plot the points $(1, 0)$ and $(a, 1)$.

Finally, it is easier to plug in a value for $f(x)$ and solve for x rather than attempting to solve for $f(x)$. Plug in one or two values for $f(x)$, plot those points and trace the graph:

$2 = \log_4 x$

$4^2 = x$

$16 = x \rightarrow$ **(16, 2)**

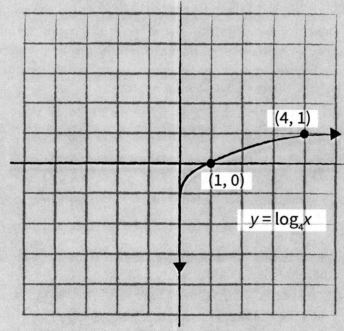

Given $f(x) = \log_{\frac{1}{3}} x$ solve for $f(81)$.

Rewrite the function in exponent form:

$x = \frac{1}{3}^{f(x)}$

$81 = \frac{1}{3}^{f(x)}$

The question is asking: to what power must you raise $\frac{1}{3}$ to get 81?

Recognize that $3^4 = 81$, so $\frac{1}{3}^4 = \frac{1}{81}$

Switch the sign of the exponent to flip the numerator and denominator:

$$\frac{1}{3}^{-4} = \frac{81}{1}$$

$$f(81) = -4$$

Arithmetic and Geometric Sequences

SEQUENCES are patterns of numbers. In most questions about sequences you must determine the pattern. In an ARITHMETIC SEQUENCE, add or subtract the same number between terms. In a GEOMETRIC SEQUENCE, multiply or divide by the same number between terms. For example, 2, 6, 10, 14, 18 and 11, 4, −3, −10, −17 are arithmetic sequences because you add 4 to each term in the first example and you subtract 7 from each term in the second example. The sequence 5, 15, 45, 135 is a geometric sequence because you multiply each term by 3. In arithmetic sequences, the number by which you add or subtract is called the COMMON DIFFERENCE. In geometric sequences, the number by which you multiply or divide is called the COMMON RATIO.

In an arithmetic sequence, the nth term (a_n) can be found by calculating $a_n = a_1 + (n-1)d$, where d is the common difference and a_1 is the first term in the sequence. In a geometric sequence, $a_n = a_1(r^n)$, where r is the common ratio.

 EXAMPLES

Find the common difference and the next term of the following sequence: 5, −1, −7, −13

Find the difference between two terms that are next to each other:

5 − (−1) = − 6

The common difference is −6. (It must be negative to show the difference is subtracted, not added.)

Now subtract 6 from the last term to find the next term:

−13 − 6 = − 19

The next term is −19.

Find the 12th term of the following sequence: 2, 6, 18, 54

First, decide whether this is an arithmetic or geometric sequence. Since the numbers are getting farther and farther apart, you know this must be a geometric sequence.

Divide one term by the term before it to find the common ratio:

18 ÷ 6 = 3

Next, plug in the common ratio and the first term to the equation $a_n = a_1(r^n)$:

$a_{12} = 2(3^{12})$

$\mathbf{a_{12} = 1{,}062{,}882}$

Notice that it would have taken a very long time to multiply each term by 3 until you got the 12th term – this is where that equation comes in handy!

The fourth term of a sequence is 9. The common difference is 11. What is the 10th term?

To answer this question, you can simply add $9 + 11 = 20$ to get the 5th term, $20 + 11 = 31$ to get the 6th term, and so on until you get the 10th term. Or you can plug the information you know into your equation $a_n = a_1 + (n - 1)d$. In this case, you do not know the first term. If you use the fourth term instead, you must replace $(n - 1)$ with $(n - 4)$:

$a_{10} = 9 + (10 - 4)11$

$\mathbf{a_{10} = 75}$

Absolute Value

The **ABSOLUTE VALUE** of a number (represented by the symbol $||$) is its distance from zero, not its value. For example, $|3| = 3$, and $|-3| = 3$ because both 3 and -3 are three units from zero. The absolute value of a number is always positive.

Equations with absolute values will have two answers, so you need to set up two equations. The first is simply the equation with the absolute value symbol removed. For the second equation, isolate the absolute value on one side of the equation and multiply the other side of the equation by -1.

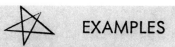 EXAMPLES

Solve for x: $|2x - 3| = x + 1$

Set up the first equation by removing the absolute value symbol then solve for x:

$|2x - 3| = x + 1$

$2x - 3 = x + 1$

$x = 4$

For the second equation, remove the absolute value and multiply by -1:

$|2x - 3| = x + 1 \rightarrow$

$2x - 3 = -(x + 1) \rightarrow$

$2x - 3 = -x - 1 \rightarrow$

$3x = 2$

$x = \frac{2}{3}$

Both answers are correct, so the complete answer is **$x = 4$ or $\frac{2}{3}$.**

Solve for y: $2|y + 4| = 10$

Set up the first equation:

$2(y + 4) = 10$

$y + 4 = 5$

$y = 1$

Set up the second equation. Remember to isolate the absolute value before multiplying by -1:

$2 |y + 4| = 10 \rightarrow$

$|y + 4| = 5 \rightarrow$

$y + 4 = -5$

$y = -9$

$y = 1$ or -9

Matrices

A **MATRIX** is an array of numbers aligned into horizontal rows and vertical columns. A matrix is described by the number of rows (m) and columns (n) it contains. For example, a matrix with 3 rows and 4 columns is a 3 × 4 matrix, as shown on the following page.

$$\begin{bmatrix} 2 & -3 & 5 & 0 \\ 4 & -6 & 2 & 11 \\ 3.5 & 7 & 2.78 & -1.2 \end{bmatrix}$$

To add or subtract 2 matrices, simply add or subtract the corresponding numbers in each matrix. Only matrices with the same dimensions can be added or subtracted, and the resulting matrix will also have the same dimensions.

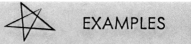 EXAMPLES

Simplify: $\begin{bmatrix} 6 & 4 & -8 \\ -3 & 1 & 0 \end{bmatrix} + \begin{bmatrix} 5 & -3 & -2 \\ -3 & 4 & 9 \end{bmatrix}$

Add each corresponding number:

$$\begin{bmatrix} 6+5 & 4+(-3) & (-8)+(-2) \\ (-3)+(-3) & 1+4 & 0+9 \end{bmatrix} = \begin{bmatrix} \mathbf{11} & \mathbf{1} & \mathbf{-10} \\ \mathbf{-6} & \mathbf{5} & \mathbf{9} \end{bmatrix}$$

Solve for x and y: $\begin{bmatrix} x & 6 \\ 4 & y \end{bmatrix} + \begin{bmatrix} 3 & 2 \\ 8 & -1 \end{bmatrix} = \begin{bmatrix} 11 & 8 \\ 12 & 4 \end{bmatrix}$

Add each corresponding number to create 2 equations:

$$\begin{bmatrix} x+3 & 6+2 \\ 4+8 & y+(-1) \end{bmatrix} = \begin{bmatrix} 11 & 8 \\ 12 & 4 \end{bmatrix}$$

$x + 3 = 11$
$y - 1 = 4$
Now, solve each equation:
$x = 8, y = 5$

In order to multiple 2 matrices, the number of columns in the first must equal the number of rows in the second. To multiply the matrices, multiply the numbers in each row of the first by the numbers in the column of the second and add. The resulting matrix will have the same number of rows as the first matrix and same number of columns as the second. Note that the order of the matrices is important when they're being multiplied: **AB** is not the same as **BA**.

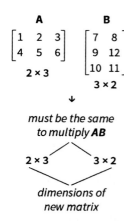

Figure 2.2. Matrix Multiplication

To multiply a matrix by a single number or variable, simply multiple each value within the matrix by that number or variable.

EXAMPLES

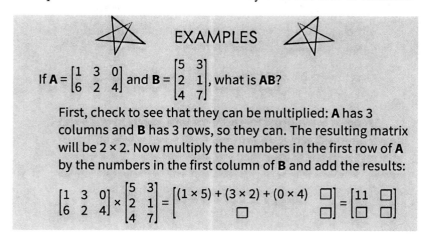

If $\mathbf{A} = \begin{bmatrix} 1 & 3 & 0 \\ 6 & 2 & 4 \end{bmatrix}$ and $\mathbf{B} = \begin{bmatrix} 5 & 3 \\ 2 & 1 \\ 4 & 7 \end{bmatrix}$, what is **AB**?

First, check to see that they can be multiplied: **A** has 3 columns and **B** has 3 rows, so they can. The resulting matrix will be 2 × 2. Now multiply the numbers in the first row of **A** by the numbers in the first column of **B** and add the results:

$$\begin{bmatrix} 1 & 3 & 0 \\ 6 & 2 & 4 \end{bmatrix} \times \begin{bmatrix} 5 & 3 \\ 2 & 1 \\ 4 & 7 \end{bmatrix} = \begin{bmatrix} (1 \times 5) + (3 \times 2) + (0 \times 4) & \square \\ \square & \square \end{bmatrix} = \begin{bmatrix} 11 & \square \\ \square & \square \end{bmatrix}$$

GO ON

Now, multiply and add to find the 3 missing values:

$$\begin{bmatrix} 1 & 3 & 0 \\ 6 & 2 & 4 \end{bmatrix} \times \begin{bmatrix} 5 & 3 \\ 2 & 1 \\ 4 & 7 \end{bmatrix} =$$

$$\begin{bmatrix} (1 \times 5) + (3 \times 2) + (0 \times 4) & (1 \times 3) + (3 \times 1) + (0 \times 7) \\ (6 \times 5) + (2 \times 2) + (4 \times 4) & (6 \times 3) + (2 \times 1) + (4 \times 7) \end{bmatrix} = \begin{bmatrix} 11 & 6 \\ 50 & 48 \end{bmatrix}$$

Simplify: $6x \begin{bmatrix} 2 & -3 \\ 6 & 4 \end{bmatrix}$

Multiply each value inside the matrix by $6x$.

$$6x \begin{bmatrix} 2 & -3 \\ 6 & 4 \end{bmatrix} = \begin{bmatrix} 6x \times 2 & 6x \times (-3) \\ 6x \times 6 & 6x \times 4 \end{bmatrix} = \begin{bmatrix} 12x & -18x \\ 36x & 24x \end{bmatrix}$$

Solving Word Problems

Any of the math concepts discussed here can be turned into a word problem, and you'll likely see word problems in various formats throughout the test. (In fact, you may have noticed that several examples in the ratio and proportion sections were word problems.)

Be sure to read the entire problem before beginning to solve it: a common mistake is to provide an answer to a question that wasn't actually asked. Also, remember that not all of the information provided in a problem is necessarily needed to solve it.

When working multiple-choice word problems like those on the ACT, it's important to check your work. Many of the incorrect answer choices will be answers that result from common mistakes. So even if a solution you calculated is listed as an answer choice, that doesn't necessarily mean you've done the problem correctly—you have to check your own answer to be sure.

The following are general steps for word problem solving:

Step 1:   Read the entire problem and determine what the question is asking.

Step 2:   List all of the given data and define the variables.

Step 3:   Determine the formula(s) needed or set up equations from the information in the problem.

Step 4:   Solve.

Step 5:   Check your answer. (Is the amount too large or small? Are the answers in the correct unit of measure?)

Word problems generally contain key words that can help you determine what math processes may be required in order to solve them.

Addition: *added, combined, increased by, in all, total, perimeter, sum,* and *more than*

Subtraction: *how much more, less than, fewer than, exceeds, difference,* and *decreased*

Multiplication: *of, times, area,* and *product*

Division: *distribute, share, average, per, out of, percent,* and *quotient*

Equals: *is, was, are, amounts to,* and *were*

Basic Word Problems

A word problem in algebra is just an equation or a set of equations described using words. Your task when solving these problems is to turn the *story* of the problem into mathematical equations.

 EXAMPLES

A store owner bought a case of 48 backpacks for $476.00. He sold 17 of the backpacks in his store for $18 each, and the rest were sold to a school for $15 each. What was the store owner's profit?

Start by listing all the data and defining the variable:

total number of backpacks = 48

cost of backpacks = $476.00

backpacks sold in store at price of $18 = 17

backpacks sold to school at a price of $15 = 48 − 17 = 31

total profit = x

Now set up an equation:

income − cost = total profit

$(306 + 465) − 476 = 295$

The store owner made a profit of **$295**.

Thirty students in Mr. Joyce's room are working on projects over 2 days. The first day, he gave them $\frac{3}{5}$ hour to work. On the second day, he gave them $\frac{1}{2}$ as much time as the first day. How much time did each student have to work on the project?

Start by listing all the data and defining your variables. Note that the number of students, while given in the problem, is not needed to find the answer:

time on 1st day = $\frac{3}{5}$ hr. = 36 min.

time on 2nd day = $\frac{1}{2}(36) = 18$ min.

total time = x

Converting units can often help you avoid operations with fractions when dealing with time.

Now set up the equation and solve:

total time = time on 1st day + time on 2nd day

$x = 36 + 18 = 54$

The students had **54 minutes** to work on the projects.

Distance Word Problems

Distance word problems involve something traveling at a constant or average speed. Whenever you read a problem that involves *how fast*, *how far*, or *for how long*, you should think of the distance equation $d = rt$, where d stands for distance, r for rate (speed), and t for time.

These problems can be solved by setting up a grid with d, r, and t along the top and each moving object on the left. When setting up the grid, make sure the units are consistent. For example, if the distance is in meters and the time is in seconds, the rate should be meters per second.

 EXAMPLES

Will drove from his home to the airport at an average speed of 30 mph. He then boarded a helicopter and flew to the hospital at an average speed of 60 mph. The entire distance was 150 miles, and the trip took 3 hours. Find the distance from the airport to the hospital.

The first step is to set up a table and fill in a value for each variable:

	d	r	t
driving	d	30	t
flying	$150 - d$	60	$3 - t$

You can now set up equations for driving and flying. The first row gives the equation $d = 30t$ and the second row gives the equation $150 - d = 60(3 - t)$.

Next, solve this system of equations. Start by substituting for d in the second equation:

$d = 30t$

$150 - d = 60(3 - t) \rightarrow 150 - 30t = 60(3 - t)$

Now solve for t:

$150 - 30t = 180 - 60t$

$-30 = -30t$

$1 = t$

Although you've solved for t, you're not done yet. Notice that the problem asks for distance. So, you need to solve for d: what the problem asked for. It does not ask for time, but you need to calculate it to solve the problem.

Driving: $30t = 30$ miles

Flying: $150 - d = 120$ miles

The distance from the airport to the hospital is 120 miles.

Two riders on horseback start at the same time from opposite ends of a field that is 45 miles long. One horse is moving at 14 mph and the second horse is moving at 16 mph. How long after they begin will they meet?

First, set up the table. The variable for time will be the same for each, because they will have been on the field for the same amount of time when they meet:

	d	r	t
horse #1	d	14	t
horse #2	$45 - d$	16	t

Next set up two equations:

Horse #1: $d = 14t$

Horse #2: $45 - d = 16t$

Now substitute and solve:

$d = 14t$

$45 - d = 16t \rightarrow 45 - 14t = 16t$

$45 = 30t$

$t = 1.5$

They will meet 1.5 hr. after they begin.

Work Problems

WORK PROBLEMS involve situations where several people or machines are doing work at different rates. Your task is usually to figure out how long it will take these people or machines to complete a task while working together. The trick to doing work problems is to figure out how much of the project each person or machine completes in the same unit of time. For example, you might calculate how much of a wall a person can paint in 1 hour, or how many boxes an assembly line can pack in 1 minute.

The next step is to set up an equation to solve for the total time. This equation is usually similar to the equation for distance, but here *work = rate × time.*

 EXAMPLES

Bridget can clean an entire house in 12 hours while her brother Tom takes 8 hours. How long would it take for Bridget and Tom to clean 2 houses together?

The ACT will give you most formulas you need to work problems, but they won't give you the formulas for percent change or work problems.

Start by figuring out how much of a house each sibling can clean on his or her own. Bridget can clean the house in 12 hours, so she can clean $\frac{1}{12}$ of the house in an hour. Using the same logic, Tom can clean $\frac{1}{8}$ of a house in an hour.

By adding these values together, you get the fraction of the house they can clean together in an hour:

$\frac{1}{12} + \frac{1}{8} = \frac{5}{24}$

They can do $\frac{5}{24}$ of the job per hour.

Now set up variables and an equation to solve:

t = time spent cleaning (in hours)

h = number of houses cleaned = 2

work = rate × time

$h = \frac{5}{24}t \rightarrow$

$2 = \frac{5}{24}t \rightarrow$

$t = \frac{48}{5} = \mathbf{9\frac{3}{5}}$ **hr.**

Farmer Dan needs to water his cornfield. One hose can water a field 1.25 times faster than a second hose. When both hoses are running, they water the field together in 5 hours. How long would it take to water the field if only the slower hose is used?

In this problem you don't know the exact time, but you can still find the hourly rate as a variable:

The first hose completes the job in f hours, so it waters $\frac{1}{f}$ field per hour. The slower hose waters the field in $1.25f$, so it waters the field in $\frac{1}{1.25f}$ hours. Together, they take 5 hours to water the field, so they water $\frac{1}{5}$ of the field per hour.

Now you can set up the equations and solve:

$\frac{1}{f} + \frac{1}{1.25f} = \frac{1}{5} \rightarrow$

$1.25f(\frac{1}{f} + \frac{1}{1.25f}) = 1.25f(\frac{1}{5}) \rightarrow$

$1.25 + 1 = 0.25f$

$2.25 = 0.25f$

$f = 9$

The fast hose takes 9 hours to water the field. The slow hose takes 1.25(9) = **11.25 hours**.

Ben takes 2 hours to pick 500 apples, and Frank takes 3 hours to pick 450 apples. How long will they take, working together, to pick 1000 apples?

Calculate how many apples each person can pick per hour:

Ben: $\frac{500 \text{ apples}}{2 \text{ hr.}} = \frac{250 \text{ apples}}{\text{hr.}}$

Frank: $\frac{450 \text{ apples}}{3 \text{ hr.}} = \frac{150 \text{ apples}}{\text{hr.}}$

Together: $\frac{250 + 150 \text{ apples}}{\text{hr.}} = \frac{400 \text{ apples}}{\text{hr.}}$

Now set up an equation to find the time it takes to pick 1000 apples:

$$\text{total time} = \frac{1 \text{ hr.}}{400 \text{ apples}} \times 1000 \text{ apples} = \frac{1000}{400} \text{ hr.} = \textbf{2.5 hours}$$

Properties of Shapes

Area and Perimeter

AREA and PERIMETER problems require you to use the equations shown in the table below to find either the area inside a shape or the distance around it (the perimeter). These equations will not be given on the test, so you need to have them memorized on test day.

Table 2.4. Area and Perimeter Equations

SHAPE	AREA	PERIMETER
circle	$A = \pi r^2$	$C = 2\pi r = \pi d$
triangle	$A = \frac{b \times h}{2}$	$P = s_1 + s_2 + s_3$
square	$A = s^2$	$P = 4s$
rectangle	$A = l \times w$	$P = 2l + 2w$

 EXAMPLES

A farmer has purchased 100 meters of fencing to enclose his rectangular garden. If one side of the garden is 20 meters long and the other is 28 meters long, how much fencing will the farmer have left over?

The perimeter of a rectangle is equal to twice its length plus twice its width:

$P = 2(20) + 2(28) = 96 \text{ m}$

The farmer has 100 meters of fencing, so he'll have $100 - 96 = \textbf{4 meters}$ left.

Taylor is going to paint a square wall that is 3.5 meters high. What is the area that Taylor will be painting?

Each side of the square wall is 3.5 meters:

$A = 3.5^2 = \textbf{12.25 m}^2$

Volume

Volume is the amount of space taken up by a three-dimensional object. Different formulas are used to find the volumes of different shapes.

Table 2.5. Volume Formulas

SHAPE	VOLUME
cylinder	$V = \pi r^2 h$
pyramid	$V = \frac{l \times w \times h}{3}$
cone	$V = \frac{\pi r^2 h}{3}$
sphere	$V = \frac{4}{3}\pi r^3$

 EXAMPLES

Charlotte wants to fill her circular swimming pool with water. The pool has a diameter of 6 meters and is 1 meter deep. How many cubic meters of water will she need to fill the pool?

This question is asking about the volume of Charlotte's pool. The circular pool is actually a cylinder, so use the formula for a cylinder: $V = \pi r^2 h$.

The diameter is 6 meters. The radius is half the diameter so $r = 6 \div 2 = 3$ meters.

Now solve for the volume:

$V = \pi r^2 h$

$V = \pi (3\text{ m})^2 (1\text{ m})$

$V = 28.3\text{ m}^3$

Charlotte will need approximately **28.3 cubic meters** of water to fill her pool.

Danny has a fishbowl that is filled to the brim with water, and purchased some spherical glass marbles to line the bottom of it. He dropped in four marbles, and water spilled out of the fishbowl. If the radius of each marble is 1 centimeter, how much water spilled?

Since the fishbowl was filled to the brim, the volume of the water that spilled out of it is equal to the volume of the marbles that Danny dropped into it. First, find the volume of one marble using the equation for a sphere:

$V = \frac{4}{3}\pi r^3$

$V = \frac{4}{3}\pi (1\text{ cm})^3$

$V = 4.2\text{ cm}^3$

Since Danny dropped in 4 marbles, multiply this volume by 4 to find the total volume:

$4.2\text{ cm}^3 \times 4 = 16.8\text{ cm}^3$

Approximately **16.8 cubic centimeters** of water spilled out of the fishbowl.

Circles

The definition of a circle is the set of points that are equal distance from a center point. The distance from the center to any given point on the circle is the RADIUS. If you draw a straight line segment across the circle going through the center, the distance along the line segment from one side of the circle to the other is called the DIAMETER. The radius is always equal to half the diameter:

$$d = 2r$$

A CENTRAL ANGLE is formed by drawing radii out from the center to two points A and B along the circle. The INTERCEPTED ARC is the portion of the circle (the arc length) between points A and B. You can find the intercepted arc length l if you know the central angle θ and vice versa:

$$l = 2\pi r \frac{\theta}{360°} \text{ffd}$$

A CHORD is a line segment that connects two points on a circle. Unlike the diameter, a chord does not have to go through the center. You can find the chord length if you know either the central angle θ or the radius of the circle r and the distance from the center of the circle to the chord d (d must be at a right angle to the chord):

If you know the central angle, chord length = $2r\sin\frac{\theta}{2}$

If you know the radius and distance, chord length = $2\sqrt{r^2 - d^2}$

A SECANT is similar to a chord; it connects two points on a circle. The difference is that a secant is a line, not a line segment, so it extends outside of the circle on either side.

A TANGENT is a straight line that touches a circle at only one point.

A SECTOR is the area within a circle that is enclosed by a central angle; if a circle is a pie, a sector is the piece of pie cut by two radii. You can find the AREA OF A SECTOR if you know either the central angle θ or the arc length l.

If you know the central angle, the area of the sector = $\pi r \frac{\theta}{360°}$

If you know the arc length, the area of a sector = $\frac{1}{2}rl$

There are two other types of angles you can create in or around a circle. INSCRIBED ANGLES are *inside* the circle: the vertex is a point P on the circle and the rays extend to two other points on the circle (A and B). As long as A and B remain constant, you can move the vertex P anywhere along the circle and the inscribed angle will be the same. CIRCUMSCRIBED ANGLES are *outside* of the circle: the rays are formed by two tangent lines that touch the circle at points A and B.

You can find the inscribed angle if you know the radius of the circle *r* and the arc length *l* between *A* and *B*:

inscribed angle $= \frac{90°l}{\pi r}$

To find the circumscribed angle, find the central angle formed by the same points *A* and *B* and subtract that angle from 180°.

 EXAMPLES

A circle has a diameter of 10 centimeters. What is the intercepted arc length between points *A* and *B* if the central angle between those points measures 46°?

First divide the diameter by two to find the radius:

$r = 10 \text{ cm} \div 2 = 5 \text{ cm}$

Now use the formula for intercepted arc length:

$l = 2\pi r \frac{\theta}{360°}$

$l = 2\pi (5 \text{ cm}) \frac{46°}{360°}$

$l = 4.0 \text{ cm}$

A chord is formed by line segment $\overline{QP}$. The radius of the circle is 5 cm and the chord length is 6 cm. Find the distance from center *C* to the chord.

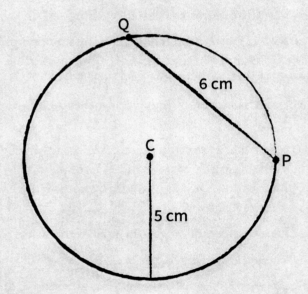

Use the formula for chord length:

chord length $= 2\sqrt{r^2 - d^2}$

In this example, we are told the chord length and the radius, and we need to solve for *d*:

$6 \text{ cm} = 2\sqrt{(5 \text{ cm})^2 - d^2}$

$3 \text{ cm} = \sqrt{(5 \text{ cm})^2 - d^2}$

$9 \text{ cm}^2 = 25 \text{ cm}^2 - d^2$

$d^2 = 16 \text{ cm}^2$

$d = \textbf{4 cm}$

Points A and B are located on a circle. The arc length between A and B is 2 centimeters. The diameter of the circle is 8 centimeters. Find the inscribed angle.

First, divide the diameter by two to find the radius:

$r = \frac{1}{2}(8 \text{ cm})$

$r = 4 \text{ cm}$

Now use the formula for an inscribed angle:

inscribed angle $= \frac{90°l}{\pi r}$

insribed angle $= \frac{90°(2 \text{ cm})}{\pi(4 \text{ cm})}$

inscribed angle = 14.3°

Congruence

CONGRUENCE means having the same size and shape. Two shapes are congruent if you can turn (rotate), flip (reflect), and/or slide (translate) one to fit perfectly on top of the other. Two angles are congruent if they measure the same number of degrees; they do not have to face the same direction nor must they necessarily have rays of equal length. If two triangles have one of the combinations of congruent sides and/or angles listed below, then those triangles are congruent:

- **SSS** – *side, side, side*
- **ASA** – *angle, side, angle*
- **SAS** – *side, angle, side*
- **AAS** – *angle, angle, side*

There are a number of common sets of congruent angles in geometry. An ISOSCELES TRIANGLE has two sides of equal length (called the legs) and two congruent angles. If you bisect an isosceles triangle by drawing a line perpendicular to the third side (called the base), you will form two congruent right triangles.

Where two lines cross and form an X, the opposite angles are congruent and are called VERTICAL ANGLES. PARALLEL LINES are lines that never cross; if you cut two parallel lines by a transversal, you will form four pairs of congruent CORRESPONDING ANGLES.

A PARALLELOGRAM is a quadrilateral in which both pairs of opposite sides are parallel and congruent (of equal length). In a parallelogram, the two pairs of opposite angles are also congruent. If you divide a parallelogram by either of the diagonals, you will form two congruent triangles.

Kate and Emily set out for a bike ride together from their house. They ride 6 miles north, then Kate turns 30° to the west and Emily turns 30° to the east. They both ride another 8 miles. If Kate rides 12 miles to return home, how far must Emily ride to get home?

Draw out Kate's and Emily's trips to see that they form triangles. The triangles have corresponding sides with lengths of 6 miles and 8 miles, and a corresponding angle in between of 120°. This fits the "SAS" rule so the triangles must be congruent. The length Kate has to ride home corresponds to the length Emily has to ride home, so **Emily must ride 12 miles**.

Angle *A* measures 53°. Find angle *H*.

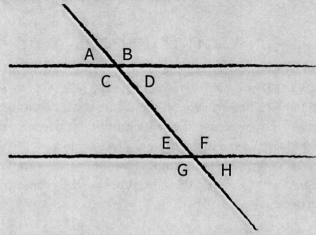

For parallel lines cut by a transversal, look for vertical and corresponding angles.

Angles *A* and *D* are vertical angles, so angle *D* must be congruent to angle *A*. Angle *D* = 53°.

Angles *D* and *H* are corresponding angles, so angle *H* must be congruent to angle *D*. **Angle H = 53°.**

Right Triangles and Trigonometry

Pythagorean Theorem

Shapes with 3 sides are known as TRIANGLES. In addition to knowing the formulas for their area and perimeter, you should also know the Pythagorean Theorem, which describes the relationship between the three sides (*a*, *b*, and *c*) of a triangle:

$$a^2 + b^2 = c^2$$

EXAMPLES

Erica is going to run a race in which she'll run 3 miles due north and 4 miles due east. She'll then run back to the starting line. How far will she run during this race?

Start by drawing a picture of Erica's route.

One leg of the triangle is missing, but you can find its length using the Pythagorean Theorem:

$a^2 + b^2 = c^2$

$3^2 + 4^2 = c^2$

$25 = c^2$

$c = 5$

Adding all 3 sides gives the length of the whole race:

$3 + 4 + 5 = $ **12 mi**

Trigonometry

Using **TRIGONOMETRY**, you can calculate an angle in a right triangle based on the ratio of two sides of that triangle. You can also calculate one of the side lengths using the measure of an angle and another side. **SINE (SIN)**, **COSINE (COS)**, and **TANGENT (TAN)** correspond to the three possible ratios of side lengths. They are defined below:

$$\sin \theta = \frac{opposite}{hypotenuse}$$

$$\cos \theta = \frac{adjacent}{hypotenuse}$$

$$\tan \theta = \frac{opposite}{adjacent}$$

Opposite is the side opposite from the angle θ, *adjacent* is the side adjacent to the angle θ, and *hypotenuse* is the longest side of the triangle, opposite from the right angle. SOH-CAH-TOA is an acronym to help you remember which ratio goes with which function.

When solving for a side or an angle in a right triangle, first identify which function to use based on the known lengths or angle.

 EXAMPLES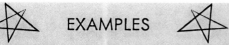

Phil is hanging holiday lights. To do so safely, he must lean his 20-foot ladder against the outside of his house an angle of 15° or less. How far from the house he can safely place the base of the ladder?

GO ON

Draw a triangle with the known length and angle labeled.

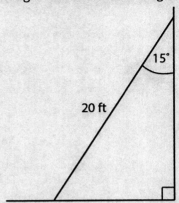

The known side (the length of the ladder) is the hypotenuse of the triangle, and the unknown distance is the side opposite the angle. Therefore, you can use sine:

$$\sin\theta = \frac{opposite}{hypotenuse}$$

$$\sin 15° = \frac{opposite}{20 \text{ feet}}$$

Now solve for the opposite side:

$$opposite = \sin 15°(20 \text{ feet})$$

$$opposite = \textbf{5.2 feet}$$

Grace is practicing shooting hoops. She is 5 feet 4 inches tall; her basketball hoop is 10 feet high. From 8 feet away, at what angle does she have to look up to see the hoop? Assume that her eyes are 4 inches lower than the top of her head.

Draw a diagram and notice that the line from Grace's eyes to the hoop of the basket forms the hypotenuse of a right triangle. The side adjacent to the angle of her eyes is the distance from the basket: 8 feet. The side opposite to Grace's eyes is the difference between the height of her eyes and the height of the basket: 10 feet − 5 feet = 5 feet.

Next, use the formula for tangent to solve for the angle:

$$\tan\theta = \frac{opposite}{adjacent}$$

$$\tan\theta = \frac{5 \text{ ft}}{8 \text{ ft}}$$

Now take the inverse tangent of both sides to solve for the angle:

$$\theta = \tan^{-1}\frac{5}{8}$$

$$\theta = \textbf{32°}$$

Coordinate Geometry

Coordinate geometry is the study of points, lines, and shapes that have been graphed on a set of axes.

Points, Lines, and Planes

In coordinate geometry, points are plotted on a **COORDINATE PLANE**, a two-dimensional plane in which the *x*-**AXIS** indicates horizontal direction and the *y*-**AXIS** indicates vertical direction. The intersection of these two axes is the **ORIGIN**. Points are defined by their location in relation to the horizontal and vertical axes. The coordinates of a point are written **(X, Y)**. The coordinates of the origin are $(0, 0)$. The *x*-coordinates to the right of the origin and the *y*-coordinates above it are positive; the *x*-coordinates to the left of the origin and the *y*-coordinates below it are negative.

A **LINE** is formed by connecting any two points on a coordinate plane; lines are continuous in both directions. Lines can be defined by their **SLOPE**, or steepness, and their *y*-**INTERCEPT**, or the point at which they intersect the *y*-axis. A line is represented by the equation $y = mx + b$. The constant *m* represents slope and the constant *b* represents the *y*-intercept.

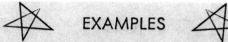 EXAMPLES

Matt parks his car near a forest where he goes hiking. From his car he hikes 1 mile north, 2 miles east, then 3 miles west. If his car represents the origin, find the coordinates of Matt's current location.

To find the coordinates, you must find Matt's displacement along the *x*- and *y*-axes. Matt hiked 1 mile north and zero miles south, so his displacement along the *y*-axis is +1 mile. Matt hiked 2 miles east and 3 miles west, so his displacement along the *x*-axis is + 2 miles − 3 miles = −1 mile.

Matt's coordinates are (−1, 1).

A square is drawn on a coordinate plane. The bottom corners are located at (−2, 3) and (4, 3). What are the coordinates for the top right corner?

Draw the coordinate plane and plot the given points. If you connect these points you will see that the bottom side is 6 units long. Since it is a square, all sides must be 6 units long. Count 6 units up from the point (4, 3) to find the top right corner.

The coordinates for the top right corner are (4, 9).

The Distance and Midpoint Formulas

To determine the distance between the points (x_1, y_1) and (x_2, y_2) from a grid use the formula:

$$d = \sqrt{(x_2 - x_1)^2 + (y_2 - y_1)^2}.$$

The midpoint, which is halfway between the 2 points, is the point:

$$\left(\frac{x_1 + x_2}{2}, \frac{y_1 + y_2}{2}\right).$$

 EXAMPLES

What is the distance between points (3, −6) and (−5, 2)?

Plug the values for $x_1, x_2, y_1,$ and y_2 into the distance formula and simplify:

$$d = \sqrt{(-5 - 3)^2 + (2 - (-6))^2} = \sqrt{64 + 64} = \sqrt{64 \times 2} = \mathbf{8\sqrt{2}}$$

What is the midpoint between points (3, −6) and (−5, 2)?

Plug the values for $x_1, x_2, y_1,$ and y_2 into the midpoint formula and simplify:

$$midpoint = \left(\frac{3 + (-5)}{2}, \frac{(-6) + 2}{2}\right) = \left(\frac{-2}{2}, \frac{-4}{2}\right) = \mathbf{(-1, -2)}$$

Describing Sets of Data

STATISTICS is the study of sets of data. The goal of statistics is to take a group of values—numerical answers from a survey, for example—and look for patterns in how that data is distributed.

When looking at a set of data, it's helpful to consider the MEASURES OF CENTRAL TENDENCY, a group of values that describe the central or typical data point from the set. The ACT covers three measures of central tendency: mean, median, and mode.

MEAN is the mathematical term for *average*. To find the mean, total all the terms and divide by the number of terms. The MEDIAN is the middle number of a given set. To find the median, put the terms in numerical order; the middle number will be the median. In the case of a set of even numbers, the middle two numbers are averaged. MODE is the number which occurs most frequently within a given set. If two different numbers both appear with the highest frequency, they are both the mode.

When examining a data set, also consider MEASURES OF VARIABILITY, which describe how the data is dispersed around the central data point. The ACT covers two measures of variability: range and standard deviation. RANGE is simply the difference between the largest and smallest values in the set. STANDARD DEVIATION is a measure of how dispersed the data is, or how far it reaches from the mean.

EXAMPLES

Find the mean of 24, 27, and 18.

Add the terms, then divide by the number of terms:

mean $= \dfrac{24 + 27 + 18}{3} = $ **23**

The mean of three numbers is 45. If two of the numbers are 38 and 43, what is the third number?

Set up the equation for mean with x representing the third number, then solve:

$mean = \dfrac{38 + 43 + x}{3} = 45$

$\dfrac{38 + 43 + x}{3} = 45$

$38 + 43 + x = 135$

$x =$ **54**

What is the median of 24, 27, and 18?

Place the terms in order, then pick the middle term:

18, 24, 27

The median is **24**.

What is the median of 24, 27, 18, and 19?

Place the terms in order. Because there is an even number of terms, the median will be the average of the middle 2 terms:

18, 19, 24, 27

$median = \dfrac{19 + 24}{2} = $ **21.5**

What is the mode of 2, 5, 4, 4, 3, 2, 8, 9, 2, 7, 2, and 2?

The mode is **2** because it appears the most within the set.

What is the standard deviation of 62, 63, 61, and 66?

To find the standard deviation, first find the mean:

$mean = \dfrac{62 + 63 + 61 + 66}{4} = 63$

Next, find the difference between each term and the mean, and square that number:

$63 - 62 = 1 \to 1^2 = 1$

$63 - 63 = 0 \to 0^2 = 0$

$63 - 61 = 2 \to 2^2 = 4$

$63 - 66 = -3 \to (-3)^2 = 9$

GO ON

Now, find the mean of the squares:

$$\text{mean} = \frac{1+0+4+9}{4} = 3.5$$

Finally, find the square root of the mean:

$$\sqrt{3.5} = 1.87$$

The standard deviation is **1.87**.

Graphs and Charts

These questions require you to interpret information from graphs and charts; they are pretty straightforward as long as you pay careful attention to detail. There are several different graph and chart types that may appear on the ACT.

Pie Charts

PIE CHARTS present parts of a whole, and are often used with percentages. Together, all the slices of the pie add up to the total number of items, or 100%.

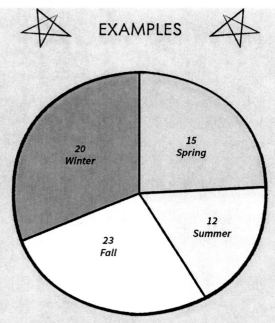

EXAMPLES

Distribution of Students' Birthdays

The pie chart above shows the distribution of birthdays in a class of students. How many students have birthdays in the spring or summer?

15 students have birthdays in the spring and 12 in winter, so there are **27 students** with birthdays in spring or summer.

Using the same graph above, what percentage of students have birthdays in winter?

Use the equation for percent:

$$\text{percent} = \frac{\text{part}}{\text{whole}} = \frac{\text{winter birthdays}}{\text{total birthdays}} \rightarrow$$

$$\frac{20}{20 + 15 + 23 + 12} = \frac{20}{70} = \frac{2}{7} = .286 \text{ or } \mathbf{28.6\%}$$

Bar Graphs

BAR GRAPHS present the numbers of an item that exist in different categories. The categories are shown on the x-axis, and the number of items is shown on the y-axis. Bar graphs are usually used to easily compare amounts.

EXAMPLES

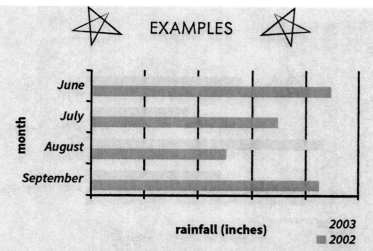

The chart above shows rainfall in inches per month. Which month had the least amount of rainfall? Which had the most?

The shortest bar will be the month that had the least rain, and the longest bar will correspond to the month with the greatest amount: **July 2003 had the least**, and **June 2002 had the most**.

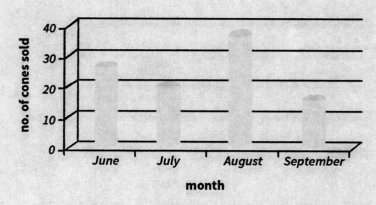

Using the chart above, how many more ice cream cones were sold in July than in September?

Line Graphs

LINE GRAPHS show trends over time. The number of each item represented by the graph will be on the *y*-axis, and time will be on the *x*-axis.

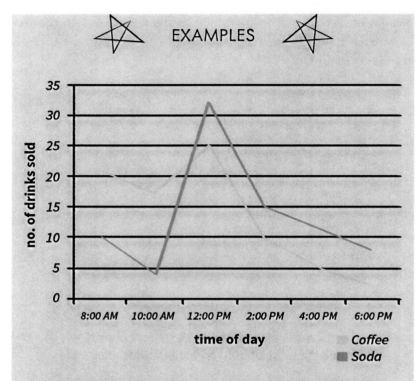

The line graph above shows beverage sales at an airport snack shop throughout the day. Which beverage sold more at 4:00 p.m.?

At 4:00 p.m., approximately 12 sodas and 5 coffees were sold, so more **soda** was sold.

At what time of day were the most beverages sold?

This question is asking for the time of day with the most sales of coffee and soda combined. It is not necessary to add up sales at each time of day to find the answer. Just from looking at the graph, you can see that sales for both beverages were highest at noon, so the answer must be **12:00 p.m.**

Histograms

A HISTOGRAM shows a distribution of types within a whole in bar chart form. While they look like bar graphs, they are more similar to pie charts: they show you parts of a whole.

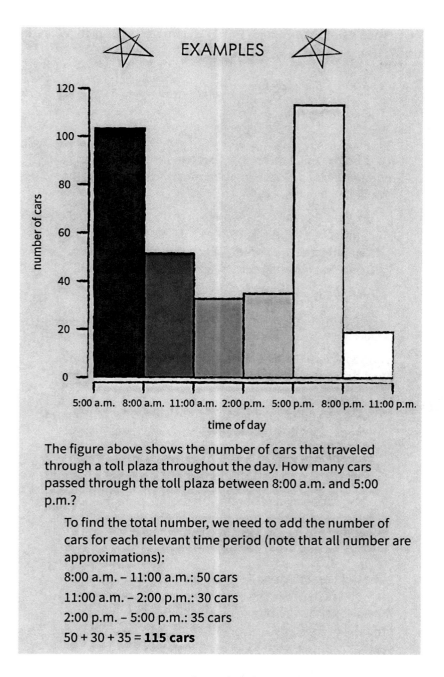

The figure above shows the number of cars that traveled through a toll plaza throughout the day. How many cars passed through the toll plaza between 8:00 a.m. and 5:00 p.m.?

To find the total number, we need to add the number of cars for each relevant time period (note that all number are approximations):

8:00 a.m. – 11:00 a.m.: 50 cars

11:00 a.m. – 2:00 p.m.: 30 cars

2:00 p.m. – 5:00 p.m.: 35 cars

50 + 30 + 35 = **115 cars**

Probability

PROBABILITY is the likelihood that an event will take place. This likelihood is expressed as a value between 0 and 1. The closer the probability is to zero, the less likely the event is to occur; the closer the probability is to 1, the more likely it is to occur.

Probability of a Single Event

The probability of an outcome occurring is found by dividing the number of desired outcomes by the number of total possible outcomes. As with percentages, a probability is the ratio of a part to a whole, with the whole being the total number of possibilities, and the part being the number of desired results. Probabilities can be written using percentages (40%), decimals (0.4), fractions, or in words (the probability of an outcome is 2 in 5).

$$probability = \frac{desired\ outcomes}{total\ possible\ outcomes}$$

 EXAMPLES

A bag holds 3 blue marbles, 5 green marbles, and 7 red marbles. If you pick one marble from the bag, what is the probability it will be blue?

> Because there are 15 marbles in the bag (3 + 5 + 7), the total number of possible outcomes is 15. Of those outcomes, 3 would be blue marbles, which is the desired outcome. Using that information, you can set up an equation:
>
> $$probability = \frac{desired\ outcomes}{total\ possible\ outcomes} = \frac{3}{15} = \frac{1}{5}$$
>
> The probability is **1 in 5 or 0.2** that a blue marble is picked.

A bag contains 75 balls. If the probability is 0.6 that a ball selected from the bag will be red, how many red balls are in the bag?

> Because you're solving for desired outcomes (the number of red balls), first you need to rearrange the equation:
>
> $$probability = \frac{desired\ outcomes}{total\ possible\ outcomes} \rightarrow$$
>
> *desired outcomes = probability × total possible outcomes*
>
> Here, choosing a red ball is the desired outcome; the total possible outcomes are represented by the 75 total balls. There are **45 red balls** in the bag.

A theater has 230 seats: 75 seats are in the orchestra area, 100 seats are in the mezzanine, and 55 seats are in the balcony. If a ticket is selected at random, what is the probability that it will be for either a mezzanine or balcony seat?

> In this problem, the desired outcome is a seat in either the mezzanine or balcony area, and the total possible outcomes are represented by the 230 total seats. So you can write this equation:
>
> $$probability = \frac{desired\ outcomes}{total\ possible\ outcomes} = 100 + 55/230 = \mathbf{0.67}$$

The probability of selecting a student whose name begins with the letter *S* from a school attendance log is 7%. If there are 42 students whose names begin with *S* enrolled at the school, how many students in total attend it?

> Because you're solving for total possible outcomes (total number of students), first you need to rearrange the equation:

Conditional Probability

CONDITIONAL PROBABILITY refers to the chances of one event occurring, given that another event has already occurred. INDEPENDENT EVENTS are events that have no effect on one another. The classic example is flipping a coin: whether you flip heads or tails one time has no bearing on how you might flip the next time. Your chance of flipping heads is always 50/50. DEPENDENT EVENTS, on the other hand, have an effect on the next event's probability. If you have a bag full of red and blue marbles, removing a red marble the first time will decrease the probability of picking a red marble the second time, since now there are fewer red marbles in the bag. The probability of event B occurring, given that event A has occurred, is written $P(B|A)$.

The probability of either event A or event B occurring is called the UNION of events A and B, written $A \cup B$. The probability of $A \cup B$ is equal to the <u>sum</u> of the probability of A occurring and the probability of B occurring, <u>minus</u> the probability of both A and B occurring. The probability of both A and B occurring is called the INTERSECTION of events A and B, written $A \cap B$. The probability of $A \cap B$ is equal to the <u>product</u> of the probability of A and the probability of B, given A. Review the equations for the probabilities of unions and intersections below:

$$P(A \cup B) = P(A) + P(B) - P(A \cap B)$$

$$P(A \cap B) = P(A) \times P(B|A)$$

The COMPLEMENT of an event is when the event <u>does not</u> occur. The probability of the complement of event A, written $P(A')$, is equal to $1 - P(A)$.

 EXAMPLES

A bag contains 5 red marbles and 11 blue marbles. What is the probability of pulling out a blue marble, followed by a red marble?

This question is asking about an intersection of events. The equation for an intersection of events is $P(A \cap B) = P(A) \times P(B|A)$.

The first event, event *A*, is picking out a blue marble. Find *P(A)*:

$$P(A) = \frac{11 \text{ blue marbles}}{16 \text{ total marbles}} = \frac{11}{16}$$

The second event, event *B*, is picking out a red marble, now that there are 15 marbles left. Find *P(B|A)*:

$$P(B|A) = \frac{5 \text{ red marbles}}{15 \text{ total marbles}} = \frac{5}{15} = \frac{1}{3}$$

$$P(A \cap B) = P(A) \times P(B|A) = \frac{11}{16} \times \frac{1}{3} = \frac{11}{48}$$

Caroline randomly draws a playing card from a full deck. What is the chance she will select either a queen or a diamond?

This question is asking about a union of events. The equation for a union of events is
$P(A \cup B) = P(A) + P(B) - P(A \cap B).$

The first event, event *A*, is selecting a queen. Find *P(A)*:

$$P(A) = \frac{4 \text{ queens}}{52 \text{ total cards}} = \frac{4}{52}$$

The second event, event *B*, is selecting a diamond. Find *P(B)*:

$$P(B) = \frac{13 \text{ diamonds}}{52 \text{ total cards}} = \frac{13}{52}$$

Now, find the probability of selecting a queen that is also a diamond:

$$P(A \cap B) = \frac{1 \text{ diamond queen}}{52 \text{ total cards}} = \frac{1}{52}$$

$$P(A \cup B) = P(A) + P(B) - P(A \cap B) = \frac{4}{52} + \frac{13}{52} - \frac{1}{52} = \frac{16}{52} = \frac{4}{13}$$

Practice Problems

1. A car rental company charges a daily fee of $48 plus 25% of the daily fee for every hour the car is late. If you rent a car for 2 days and bring it back 2 hours late, what will be the total charge?

   A. $72

   B. $96

   C. $108

   D. $120

   E. $144

2. A car dealership has sedans, SUVs, and minivans in a ratio of 6:3:1, respectively. In total there are 200 of these vehicles on the lot. What proportion of those vehicles are sedans?

   F. $\frac{3}{100}$

   G. $\frac{3}{10}$

   H. $\frac{3}{5}$

   J. $\frac{2}{3}$

   K. $\frac{9}{10}$

3. Evaluate the expression $\frac{x^2 - 2y}{y}$ when $x = 20$ and $y = \frac{x}{2}$.

   A. 0

   B. 9

   C. 19

   D. 36

   E. 38

4. Which expression is equivalent to $x^3 - 3x^2 + (2x)^3 - x$?

   F. $20x$

   G. $6x^3$

   H. $x^3 - 3x^2 + 7x$

   J. $7x^3 - 3x^2 - x$

   K. $9x^3 - 3x^2 - x$

5. Solve for y: $10y - 8 - 2y = 4y - 22 + 5y$

   A. $y = -30$

   B. $y = -4\frac{2}{3}$

   C. $y = 14$

   D. $y = 30$

   E. $y = 30\frac{2}{3}$

6. If m represents a car's average mileage in miles per gallon, p represents the price of gas in dollars per gallon, and d represents distance in miles, which of the following algebraic equations represents the cost (c) of gas per mile?

   F. $c = \frac{p}{m}$

   G. $c = \frac{dp}{m}$

   H. $c = \frac{mp}{d}$

   J. $c = \frac{m}{p}$

   K. $c = \frac{d}{mp}$

7. What is the 10th term in the following arithmetic sequence: 20, 8, –4, –16, ...? (Note: In an arithmetic sequence, the difference between terms is constant.)

   A. –136

   B. –100

   C. –88

   D. –76

   E. –72

8. Liz is installing a tile backsplash. If each tile is an equilateral triangle with sides that measure 6 centimeters in length, how many tiles does she need to cover an area of 1800 square centimeters?

   F. 18 tiles

   G. 36 tiles

   H. 50 tiles

   J. 100 tiles

   K. 300 tiles

9. A courtyard garden has flower beds in the shape of 4 equilateral triangles arranged so that their bases enclose a square space in the middle for a fountain. If the space for the fountain has an area of 1 square meter, find the total area of the flower beds and fountain space.

A. 1.43 m²

B. 1.73 m²

C. 2.73 m²

D. 3 m²

E. 3.23 m²

10. Ed is going to fill his swimming pool with a garden hose. His neighbor, a volunteer firefighter, wants to use a fire hose attached to the hydrant in the front yard to make the job go faster. The fire hose sprays 13.5 times as much water per minute as the garden hose. If the garden hose and the fire hose together can fill the pool in 107 minutes, how long would it have taken to fill the pool with the garden hose alone?

F. 7 hours, 37.9 min

G. 7 hours, 55.6 min

H. 1 day, 4.5 min

J. 1 day, 7 hours

K. 1 day, 1 hour, 51.5 min

Mathematics Answer Key

1.	D.	**6.**	F
2.	H.	**7.**	C.
3.	E.	**8.**	J
4.	K.	**9.**	C.
5.	C.	**10.**	K

three

READING

40 questions ¦ 35 minutes

The reading test has four passages with ten questions each. There will be one passage each from four categories: Prose, Humanities, Social Studies, and Natural Science. Within each category you may also encounter two shorter passages instead of one long passage. You'll be asked questions about:

- ◆ the main idea of a passage
- ◆ supporting details in the passage
- ◆ the structure of the passage
- ◆ the author's purpose and tone
- ◆ logical inferences that can be drawn from the passage
- ◆ comparisons between passages
- ◆ vocabulary and figurative language
- ◆ fictional characters motives and actions

The questions themselves are usually not very challenging—the answers to most of them can be found by simply reading the passage thoroughly. The challenge on the Reading section comes from the short length of time you'll be given to read passages and answer questions. With only about eight minutes per passage, you need to be able to read passages quickly and pick out important information without returning to the passage over and over. Each category will require you to shift your focus slightly when reading:

- ◆ The **PROSE** fiction passages are usually excerpts from short stories or novels. You'll want to take note of the plot, characters, style, and tone.
- ◆ The **HUMANITIES** passage topics are culturally based, focusing on the arts and literature, and can be written journalistically, analytically, or as a personal essay. These tend to portray varying degrees of bias, which you will need to take into account when reading.

- The **SOCIAL STUDIES** passage topics are focused on the workings of civilizations and societies and usually have a political perspective. Take notice of dates, names, chronological order, key concepts, and cause and effect relationships. The authors tend to express controversial views about the subject. It is important that you are able to separate the author's point of view from the general argument.

- The **NATURAL SCIENCE** passages present experiments and scientific theories, along with their implications and reasoning. These are going to include considerable facts and data. Pay attention to comparisons, as well as cause and effect.

The Main Idea

The main idea of a text is the author's purpose in writing a book, article, story, etc. Being able to identify and understand the main idea is a critical skill necessary to comprehend and appreciate what you're reading.

Consider a political election. A candidate is running for office and plans to deliver a speech asserting her position on tax reform. The topic of the speech—tax reform—is clear to voters, and probably of interest to many. However, imagine that the candidate believes that taxes should be lowered. She is likely to assert this argument in her speech, supporting it with examples proving why lowering taxes would benefit the public and how it could be accomplished. While the topic of the speech would be tax reform, the benefit of lowering taxes would be the main idea. Other candidates may have different perspectives on the topic; they may believe that higher taxes are necessary, or that current taxes are adequate. It is likely that their speeches, while on the same topic of tax reform, would have different main ideas: different arguments likewise supported by different examples. Determining what a speaker, writer, or text is asserting about a specific issue will reveal the MAIN IDEA.

Topic: The subject of the passage.
Theme: An idea or concept the author refers to repeatedly.
Main idea: The argument the writer is making about the topic.

One more quick note: the exam may also ask about a passage's THEME, which is similar to but distinct from its topic. While a TOPIC is usually a specific *person, place, thing,* or *issue*, the theme is an *idea* or *concept* that the author refers back to frequently. Examples of common themes include ideas like the importance of family, the dangers of technology, and the beauty of nature.

There will be many questions on the exam that require you to differentiate between the topic, theme, and main idea of a passage. Let's look at an example:

Babe Didrikson Zaharias, one of the most decorated female athletes of the twentieth century, is an inspiration for everyone. Born in 1911 in Beaumont, Texas, Zaharias lived in a time when women were considered second-class to men, but she never let that stop her from becoming a champion. Babe was one of seven children in a poor immigrant family, and was competitive from an early age. As a child she excelled at most things she tried, especially sports, which continued into high school and beyond. After high school, Babe played amateur basketball for two years, and soon after began training in track and field. Despite the fact that women were only allowed to enter in three events, Babe represented the United States in the 1932 Los Angeles Olympics, and won two gold medals and one silver for track and field events.

In the early 1930s, Babe began playing golf which earned her a legacy. The first tournament she entered was a men's only tournament; however she did not make the cut to play. Playing golf as an amateur was the only option for a woman at this time, since there was no professional women's league. Babe played as an amateur for a little over a decade, until she turned pro in 1947 for the Ladies Professional Golf Association (LPGA) of which she was a founding member. During her career as a golfer, Babe won eighty-two tournaments, amateur and professional, including the U.S. Women's Open, All-American Open, and British Women's Open Golf Tournament. In 1953, Babe was diagnosed with cancer, but fourteen weeks later, she played in a tournament. That year she won her third U.S. Women's Open. However by 1955, she didn't have the physicality to compete anymore, and she died of the disease in 1956.

The topic of this passage is obviously Babe Zaharias—the whole passage describes events from her life. Determining the main idea, however, requires a little more analysis. The passage describes Babe Zaharias' life, but the main idea of the paragraph is what it says about her life. To figure out the main idea, consider what the writer is saying about Babe Zaharias. The writer is saying that she's someone to admire—that's the main idea and what unites all the information in the paragraph. Lastly, what might the theme of the passage be? The writer refers to several broad concepts, including never giving up and overcoming the odds, both of which could be themes of the passage.

Two major indicators of the main idea of a paragraph or passage follow below:

- It is a general idea; it applies to all the more specific ideas in the passage. Every other sentence in a paragraph should be able to relate in some way to the main idea.
- It asserts a specific viewpoint that the author supports with facts, opinions, or other details. In other words, the main idea takes a stand.

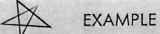

EXAMPLE

It's easy to puzzle over the landscapes of our solar system's distant planets—how could we ever know what those far-flung places really look like? However, scientists utilize a number of tools to visualize the surfaces of many planets. The topography of Venus, for example, has been explored by several space probes, including the Russian Venera landers and NASA's Magellan orbiter. These craft used imaging and radar to map the surface of the planet, identifying a whole host of features including volcanoes, craters, and a complex system of channels. Mars has likewise been mapped by space probes, including the famous Mars Rovers, which are automated vehicles that actually landed on the planet's surface. These rovers have been used by NASA and other space agencies to study the geology, climate, and possible biology of the planet.

In addition to these long-range probes, NASA has also used its series of orbiting telescopes to study distant planets. These four massively powerful telescopes include the famous Hubble Space Telescope as well as the Compton Gamma Ray Observatory, Chandra X-Ray Observatory, and the Spitzer Space Telescope. These allow scientists to examine planets using not only visible light but also infrared and near-infrared light, ultraviolet light, x-rays and gamma rays.

Powerful telescopes aren't just found in space: NASA makes use of Earth-bound telescopes as well. Scientists at the National Radio Astronomy Observatory in Charlottesville, VA, have spent decades using radio imaging to build an incredibly detailed portrait of Venus' surface. In fact, Earth-bound telescopes offer a distinct advantage over orbiting telescopes because they allow scientists to capture data from a fixed point, which in turn allows them to effectively compare data collected over a long period of time.

Which of the following sentences best describes the main idea of the passage?

- **A)** It's impossible to know what the surfaces of other planets are really like.
- **B)** Telescopes are an important tool for scientists studying planets in our solar system.
- **C)** Venus' surface has many of the same features as the Earth's, including volcanoes, craters, and channels.
- **D)** Scientists use a variety of advanced technologies to study the surface of the planets in our solar system.

Answer A) can be eliminated because it directly contradicts the rest of the passage, which goes into detail about how scientists have learned about the surfaces of other planets. Answers B) and C) can also be eliminated because they offer only specific details from the passage; while both choices contain details from the passage, neither is general enough to encompass the passage as a whole. Only answer D) provides an assertion that is both supported by the passage's content and general enough to cover the entire passage.

Topic and Summary Sentences

The main idea of a paragraph usually appears within the topic sentence. The **TOPIC SENTENCE** introduces the main idea to readers; it indicates not only the topic of a passage, but also the writer's perspective on the topic.

Notice, for example, how the first sentence in the text about Babe Zaharias states the main idea: *Babe Didrikson Zaharias, one of the most decorated female athletes of the twentieth century, is an inspiration for everyone.*

Even though paragraphs generally begin with topic sentences due to their introductory nature, on occasion writers build up to the topic sentence by using supporting details in order to generate interest or build an argument. Be alert for paragraphs when writers do not include a clear topic sentence at all; even without a clear topic sentence, a paragraph will still have a main idea. You may also see a **SUMMARY SENTENCE** at the end of a passage. As its name suggests, this sentence sums up the passage, often by restating the main idea and the author's key evidence supporting it.

 EXAMPLE

In the following paragraph, what are the topic and summary sentences?

The Constitution of the United States establishes a series of limits to rein in centralized power. Separation of powers distributes federal authority among three competing branches: the executive, the legislative, and the judicial. Checks and balances allow the branches to check the usurpation of power by any one branch. States' rights are protected under the Constitution from too much encroachment by the federal government. Enumeration of powers names the specific and few powers the federal government has. These four restrictions have helped sustain the American republic for over two centuries.

The topic sentence is the first sentence in the paragraph. It introduces the topic of discussion, in this case the constitutional limits on centralized power. The summary sentence is the last sentence in the paragraph. It sums up the information that was just presented: here, that constitutional limits have helped sustain the United States of America for over two hundred years.

Supporting Details

SUPPORTING DETAILS provide more support for the author's main idea. For instance, in the Babe Zaharias example, the writer makes the general assertion that *Babe Didrikson Zaharias, one of the most decorated female athletes of the twentieth century, is an inspiration for everyone.* The rest of the paragraph provides supporting details with facts showing why she is an inspiration: the names of the challenges she overcame, and the specific years she competed in the Olympics.

Be alert for **SIGNAL WORDS**, which indicate supporting details and so can be helpful in identifying supporting details. Signal words can also help you rule out sentences that are not the main idea or topic sentence: if a sentence begins with one of these phrases, it will likely be too specific to be a main idea.

Questions on the ACT will ask you to find details that support a particular idea and also to explain why a particular detail was included in the passage. In order to answer these questions, you must have a solid understanding of the passage's main idea. With this knowledge, you can determine how a supporting detail fits in with the larger structure of the passage.

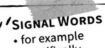

SIGNAL WORDS
- for example
- specifically
- in addition
- furthermore
- for instance
- others
- in particular
- some

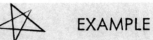 EXAMPLE

It's easy to puzzle over the landscapes of our solar system's distant planets—how could we ever know what those far-flung places really look like? However, scientists utilize a number of tools to visualize the surfaces of many planets. The topography of Venus, for example, has been explored by several space probes, including the Russian Venera landers and NASA's Magellan orbiter. These craft used imaging and radar to map the surface of the planet, identifying a whole host of features including volcanoes, craters, and a complex system of channels. Mars has likewise been mapped by space probes, including the famous Mars Rovers, which are automated vehicles that actually landed on the planet's surface. These rovers have been used by NASA and other space agencies to study the geology, climate, and possible biology of the planet.

In addition to these long-range probes, NASA has also used its series of orbiting telescopes to study distant planets. These four massively powerful telescopes include the famous Hubble Space Telescope as well as the Compton Gamma Ray Observatory, Chandra X-Ray Observatory, and the Spitzer Space Telescope. These allow scientists to examine planets using not only visible light but also infrared and near-infrared light, ultraviolet light, x-rays and gamma rays.

Powerful telescopes aren't just found in space: NASA makes use of Earth-bound telescopes as well. Scientists at the National Radio Astronomy Observatory in Charlottesville, VA, have spent decades using radio imaging to build an incredibly detailed portrait of Venus' surface. In fact, Earth-bound telescopes offer a distinct advantage over orbiting telescopes because they allow scientists to capture data from a fixed point, which in turn allows them to effectively compare data collected over a long period of time.

Which sentence from the text best develops the idea that scientists make use of many different technologies to study the surfaces of other planets?

A) These rovers have been used by NASA and other space agencies to study the geology, climate, and possible biology of the planet.

B) It's easy to puzzle over the landscapes of our solar system's distant planets—how could we ever know what those far-flung places really look like?

C) In addition these long-range probes, NASA has also used its series of orbiting telescopes to study distant planets.

D) These craft used imaging and radar to map the surface of the planet, identifying a whole host of features including volcanoes, craters, and a complex system of channels.

You're looking for detail from the passage that supports the main idea—scientists make use of many different technologies to study the surfaces of other planets. Answer A) includes a specific detail about rovers, but

does not offer any details that support the idea of multiple technologies being used. Similarly, answer D) provides another specific detail about space probes. Answer B) doesn't provide any supporting details; it simply introduces the topic of the passage. Only answer C) provides a detail that directly supports the author's assertion that scientists use multiple technologies to study the planets.

If true, which sentence could be added to the passage above to support the author's argument that scientists use many different technologies to study the surface of planets?

A) Because the Earth's atmosphere blocks x-rays, gamma rays, and infrared radiation, NASA needed to put telescopes in orbit above the atmosphere.

B) In 2015, NASA released a map of Venus which was created by compiling images from orbiting telescopes and long-range space probes.

C) NASA is currently using the Curiosity and Opportunity rovers to look for signs of ancient life on Mars.

D) NASA has spent over $2.5 billion to build, launch, and repair the Hubble Space Telescope.

You can eliminate answers C) and D) because they don't address the topic of studying the surface of planets. Answer A) can also be eliminated because it only addresses a single technology. Only choice B) would add support to the author's claim about the importance of using multiple technologies.

The author likely included the detail that *Earth-bound telescopes offer a distinct advantage over orbiting telescopes because they allow scientists to capture data from a fixed point* in order to

A) explain why it has taken scientists so long to map the surface of Venus.

B) suggest that Earth-bound telescopes are the most important equipment used by NASA scientists.

C) prove that orbiting telescopes will soon be replaced by Earth-bound telescopes.

D) demonstrate why NASA scientists rely on many different types of scientific equipment.

Only answer D) relates directly to the author's main argument. The author doesn't mention how long it has taken to map the surface of Venus (answer A), nor does he say that one technology is more important than the others (answer B). And while this detail does highlight the advantages of using Earth-bound telescopes, the author's argument is that many technologies are being used at

Text Structure

Authors can structure passages in a number of different ways. These distinct organizational patterns, referred to as **TEXT STRUCTURE**, use the logical relationships between ideas to improve the readability and coherence of a text. The most common ways passages are organized include:

- **PROBLEM-SOLUTION**: The author presents a problem and then discusses a solution.
- **COMPARISON-CONTRAST**: The author presents two situations and then discusses their similarities and differences.
- **CAUSE-EFFECT**: The author presents an action and then discusses the resulting effects.
- **DESCRIPTIVE**: The author describes an idea, object, person, or other item in detail.

 EXAMPLE

The issue of public transportation has begun to haunt the fast-growing cities of the southern United States. Unlike their northern counterparts, cities like Atlanta, Dallas, and Houston have long promoted growth out and not up—these are cities full of sprawling suburbs and single-family homes, not densely concentrated skyscrapers and apartments. What to do then, when all those suburbanites need to get into the central business districts for work? For a long time it seemed highways were the twenty-lane wide expanses of concrete that would allow commuters to move from home to work and back again. But these modern miracles have become time-sucking, pollution-spewing nightmares. They may not like it, but it's time for these cities to turn toward public transport like trains and buses if they are to remain livable.

The organization of this passage can best be described as:

A) a comparison of two similar ideas

B) a description of a place

C) a discussion of several effects all related to the same cause

D) a discussion of a problem followed by the suggestion of a solution

You can exclude answer choice C) because the author provides no root cause or a list of effects. From there this question gets tricky, because the passage contains structures similar to those described above. For example, it compares two things (cities in the North and South) and describes a place (a sprawling city). However, if you look at the overall organization of the passage, you can see that it starts by presenting a problem (transportation) and then presents a solution (trains and buses), making answer D) the only choice that encompasses the entire passage.

Understanding the Author

The Author's Purpose

Whenever an author writes a text, she always has a purpose, whether that's to entertain, inform, explain, or persuade. A short story, for example, is meant to entertain, while an online news article would be designed to inform the public about a current event. Each of these different types of writing has a specific name:

- NARRATIVE WRITING tells a story. (novel, short story, play)
- EXPOSITORY WRITING informs people. (newspaper and magazine articles)
- TECHNICAL WRITING explains something. (product manual, directions)
- PERSUASIVE WRITING tries to convince the reader of something. (opinion column on a blog)

On the exam, you may be asked to categorize a passage as one of these types, either by specifically naming it as such or by identifying its general purpose.

You may also be asked about primary and secondary sources. These terms describe not the writing itself but the author's relationship to what's being written about. A PRIMARY SOURCE is an unaltered piece of writing that was composed during the time when the events being described took place; these texts are often written by the people directly involved. A SECONDARY SOURCE might address the same topic but provide extra commentary or analysis. These texts are written by outside observers and may even be composed after the event. For example, a book written by a political candidate to inform people about his or her stand on an issue is a primary source. An online article written by a journalist analyzing how that position will affect the election is a secondary source; a book by a historian about that election would be a secondary source, too.

EXAMPLE

Elizabeth closed her eyes and braced herself on the armrests that divided her from her fellow passengers. Take-off was always the worst part for her. The revving of the engines, the way her stomach dropped as the plane lurched upward; it made her feel sick. Then, she had to watch the world fade away beneath her, getting smaller and smaller until it was just her and the clouds hurtling through the sky. Sometimes (but only sometimes) it just had to be endured, though. She focused on the thought of her sister's smiling face and her new baby nephew as the plane slowly pulled onto the runway.

The passage above is reflective of which type of writing?

A) Narrative

B) Expository

C) Technical

D) Persuasive

The passage is telling a story—we meet Elizabeth and learn about her fear of flying—so it's a narrative text, answer choice A). There is no factual information presented or explained, nor is the author trying to persuade the reader of anything.

Tone

The author of a text expresses how she feels about her subject and audience through the tone of the text. For example, a newspaper article about a prominent philanthropist might have be serious and appreciative, while a website blurb about an upcoming sale could be playful and relaxed.

Table 3.1. Tone Words

Positive	Negative	Neutral
admiring	angry	casual
approving	annoyed	detached
celebratory	belligerent	formal
comforting	bitter	impartial
confident	condescending	informal
earnest	confused	objective
encouraging	cynical	questioning
excited	depressed	unconcerned
forthright	derisive	
funny	despairing	
hopeful	disrespectful	
humorous	embarrassed	
modest	fearful	
nostalgic	gloomy	

optimistic	melancholy
playful	mournful
poignant	ominous
proud	pessimistic
relaxed	skeptical
respectful	solemn
sentimental	suspicious
silly	unsympathetic
sympathetic	

Authors signify tone in a number of ways. The main clue to look for is the author's diction, or word choice. Obviously, if the author is choosing words that have a negative connotation, then the overall tone of the text is negative, while words with a positive connotation will convey a positive tone. For example, the author of a biographical article may choose to describe his subject as *determined* or *pigheaded*; both mean similar things, but the first has a more positive connotation than the second. Literary devices such as imagery and metaphors can likewise generate a specific tone by evoking a particular feeling in the reader.

Tone is also developed by the structure of the text. Long, complicated sentences will make a passage seem formal, while short, pithy writing is more informal. Similarly, a text that cites statistical figures to support a logical argument will have a different tone that a text structured as a casual conversation between author and reader.

 EXAMPLE

It could be said that the great battle between the North and South we call the Civil War was a battle for individual identity. The states of the South had their own culture, one based on farming, independence, and the rights of both man and state to determine their own paths. Similarly, the North had forged its own identity as a center of centralized commerce and manufacturing. This clash of lifestyles was bound to create tension, and this tension was bound to lead to war. But people who try to sell you this narrative are wrong.

The tone of the passage above can best be described as

A) formal and forthright
B) casual and mournful
C) detached and solemn
D) objective and skeptical

Audience

A good author will write with a specific audience in mind. For example, an opinion column on a website might be specifically targeted toward undecided voters, or a brochure for an upcoming art exhibit might address people who have donated money to the museum in the past. The author's audience can influence what information is included in the text, the tone the author uses, and the structure of the text.

The easiest way to identify the intended audience of a text is simply to ask yourself who would benefit the most from the information in the passage. A passage about how often to change the oil in a car would provide useful information to new drivers, but likely wouldn't tell an experienced driver something she didn't already know. Thus, the audience is likely new drivers who are learning to take care of cars.

The author may also directly or indirectly refer to his audience. The author of an article on oil changes might say something like *new drivers will want to keep an eye on their mileage when deciding how often to get an oil change*, which tells the reader who the intended audience is.

 EXAMPLE

The museum's newest exhibit opens today! The Ecology of the Columbia River Basin is an exciting collaboration between the New Valley Museum of Natural Science and the U.S. Department of the Interior. The exhibit includes plants, insects, birds, and mammals that are unique to the Columbia River Basin and explores the changes that have occurred in this delicate ecosystem over the last century. The exhibit is kid friendly, with interactive, hands-on exhibits and exciting audio-visual presentations. Individual tickets are available on the museum's website, and groups may apply for special ticket prices by calling the museum directly.

The intended audience for this passage likely includes all of the following except

A) a middle school biology teacher

B) employees of the U.S. Department of the Interior

C) parents of young children

D) naturalists with an interest in local birds

The passage provides information to anyone who might be interested in an exhibit on the ecology of the Columbia River Basin. This includes biology teachers (who can get special group ticket prices), parents of young children (who now know the exhibit is kid friendly), and naturalists (who will want to see the unique birds). The only people who would not learn anything new from reading the passage are employees of the U.S. Department of the Interior (answer B), who likely already know about the exhibit since they helped create it.

Facts vs. Opinions

On the ACT you might be asked to identify a statement in a passage as either a fact or an opinion, so you'll need to know the difference between the two. A FACT is a statement or thought that can be proven to be true. The statement *Wednesday comes after Tuesday* is a fact—you can point to a calendar to prove it. In contrast, an OPINION is an assumption that is not based in fact and cannot be proven to be true. The assertion that *television is more entertaining than feature films* is an opinion—people will disagree on this, and there's no reference you can use to prove or disprove it.

 EXAMPLE

Exercise is critical for healthy development in children. Today, there is an epidemic of unhealthy children in the United States who will face health problems in adulthood due to poor diet and lack of exercise in childhood. This is a problem for all Americans, especially with the rising cost of health care.

It is vital that school systems and parents encourage their children to engage in a minimum of thirty minutes of cardiovascular exercise each day, mildly increasing their heart rate for a sustained period. This is proven to decrease the likelihood of developmental diabetes, obesity, and a multitude of other health problems. Also, children need a proper diet rich in fruits and vegetables so that they can grow and develop physically, as well as learn healthy eating habits early on.

Which of the following is a fact in the passage, not an opinion?

- **A)** Fruits and vegetables are the best way to help children be healthy.
- **B)** Children today are lazier than they were in previous generations.
- **C)** The risk of diabetes in children is reduced by physical activity.
- **D)** Children should engage in thirty minutes of exercise a day.

Choice B) can be discarded immediately because it is negative (recall that particularly negative answer statements are generally wrong) and is not discussed anywhere in the passage. Answers A) and D) are both opinions—the author is promoting exercise, fruits, and vegetables as a way to make children healthy. (Notice that these incorrect answers contain words that hint at being an opinion such as best, should, or other comparisons.) Answer B), on the other hand, is a simple fact stated by the author; it appears in the passage with the word *proven*, indicating that you don't just need to take the author's word for it.

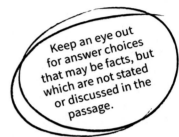

Keep an eye out for answer choices that may be facts, but which are not stated or discussed in the passage.

Drawing Conclusions

In addition to understanding the main idea and factual content of a passage, you'll also be asked to take your analysis one step further and anticipate what other information could logically be added to the passage. In a non-fiction passage, for example, you might be asked which statement the author of the passage would agree with. In an excerpt from a fictional work, you might be asked to anticipate what a character would do next.

To answer these questions, you must have a solid understanding of the topic, theme, and main idea of the passage; armed with this information, you can figure out which of the answer choices best fits within those criteria (or alternatively, which ones do not). For example, if the author of the passage is advocating for safer working conditions in textile factories, any supporting details that would be added to the passage should support that idea. You might add sentences that contain information about the number of accidents that occur in textile factories or that outline a new plan for fire safety.

GO ON

Today, there is an epidemic of unhealthy children in the United States who will face health problems in adulthood due to poor diet and lack of exercise during their childhoods. This is a problem for all Americans, as adults with chronic health issues are adding to the rising cost of healthcare. A child who grows up living an unhealthy lifestyle is likely to become an adult who does the same.

Because exercise is critical for healthy development in children, it is vital that school systems and parents encourage their children to engage in a minimum of thirty minutes of cardiovascular exercise each day. Even this small amount of exercise has been proven to decrease the likelihood that young people will develop diabetes, obesity, and other health issues as adults. In addition to exercise, children need a proper diet rich in fruits and vegetables so that they can grow and develop physically. Starting a good diet early also teaches children healthy eating habits they will carry into adulthood.

The author of this passage would most likely agree with which statement?

    A) Parents are solely responsible for the health of their children.

    B) Children who do not want to exercise should not be made to.

    C) Improved childhood nutrition will help lower the amount Americans spend on healthcare.

    D) It's not important to teach children healthy eating habits because they will learn them as adults.

The author would most likely support answer C): he mentions in the first paragraph that poor diets are adding to the rising cost of healthcare. The main idea of the passage is that nutrition and exercise are important for children, so answer B) doesn't make sense—the author would likely support measures to encourage children to exercise. Answers A) and D) can also be eliminated because they are directly contradicted in the text. The author specifically mentions the role of school systems, so he doesn't believe parents are solely responsible for their children's health. He also specifically states that children who grow up with unhealthy eating habits will become adults with unhealthy eating habits, which contradicts D).

Elizabeth closed her eyes and braced herself on the armrests that divided her from her fellow passengers. Take-off was always the worst part for her. The revving of the engines, the way her stomach dropped as the plane lurched upward; it made her feel sick. Then, she had to watch the world fade away beneath her, getting smaller and smaller until it was just her and the clouds hurtling through the sky. Sometimes (but only sometimes) it just had to be endured, though. She focused on the thought of her sister's smiling face and her new baby nephew as the plane slowly pulled onto the runway.

Which of the following is Elizabeth least likely to do in the future?

A) Take a flight to her brother's wedding.

B) Apply for a job as a flight attendant.

C) Never board an airplane again.

D) Get sick on an airplane.

It's clear from the passage that Elizabeth hates flying, but it willing to endure it for the sake of visiting her family. Thus, it seems likely that she would be willing to get on a plane for her brother's wedding, making A) and C) incorrect answers. The passage also explicitly tells us that she feels sick on planes, so D) is likely to happen. We can infer, though, that she would not enjoy being on an airplane for work, so she's very unlikely to apply for a job as a flight attendant, which is choice B).

Meaning of Words and Phrases

On the reading section you may be asked to provide definitions or intended meanings for words within passages. You may have never encountered some of these words before the test, but there are tricks you can use to figure out what they mean.

Context Clues

A fundamental vocabulary skill is using context to determine the meaning of a word. There are two types of context that can help you understand unfamiliar words: situational context and sentence context. Regardless of which context you encounter, these types of questions are not really testing your knowledge of vocabulary; rather, they test your ability to comprehend the meaning of a word through its usage.

SITUATIONAL CONTEXT helps you determine the meaning of a word through the setting or circumstances in which that word or phrase occurs. Using SENTENCE CONTEXT requires analyzing only the sentence in which the new word appears to understand it.

To figure out words using sentence context clues, you should first identify the most important words in the sentence.

There are four types of clues that can help you understand the context, and therefore the meaning of a word:

- RESTATEMENT CLUES occur when the definition of the word is clearly stated in the sentence.
- POSITIVE/NEGATIVE CLUES can tell you whether a word has a positive or negative meaning.
- CONTRAST CLUES include the opposite meaning of a word. Words like *but*, *on the other hand*, and *however* are tip-offs that a sentence contains a contrast clue.
- SPECIFIC DETAIL CLUES provide a precise detail that can help you understand the meaning of the word.

It is important to remember that more than one of these clues can be present in the same sentence. The more there are, the easier it will be to determine the meaning of the word. For example, the following sentence uses both restatement and positive/negative clues: *Janet suddenly found herself destitute, so poor she could barely afford to eat.* The second part of the sentence clearly indicates that *destitute* is a negative word. It also restates the meaning: very poor.

 EXAMPLE

I had a hard time reading her <u>illegible</u> handwriting.

A) neat
B) unsafe
C) sloppy
D) educated

Already, you know that this sentence is discussing something that is hard to read. Look at the word that illegible is describing: handwriting. Based on context clues, you can tell that illegible means that her handwriting is hard to read.

Next, look at the answer choices. Choice A), *neat*, is obviously a wrong answer because neat handwriting would not be difficult to read. Choices B) and D), *unsafe* and *educated*, don't make sense. Therefore, choice C), *sloppy*, is the best answer.

The dog was <u>dauntless</u> in the face of danger, braving the fire to save the girl trapped inside the building.

A) difficult
B) fearless
C) imaginative
D) startled

Demonstrating bravery in the face of danger would be B), fearless. In this case, the restatement clue (braving the fire) tells you exactly what the word means.

Beth did not spend any time preparing for the test, but Tyrone kept a <u>rigorous</u> study schedule.

A) strict

B) loose

C) boring

D) strange

In this case, the contrast word *but* tells us that Tyrone studied in a different way than Beth, which means it's a contrast clue. If Beth did not study hard, then Tyrone did. The best answer, therefore, is choice A).

Analyzing Words

As you no doubt know, determining the meaning of a word can be more complicated than just looking in a dictionary. A word might have more than one DENOTATION, or definition; which one the author intends can only be judged by examining the surrounding text. For example, the word *quack* can refer to the sound a duck makes, or to a person who publicly pretends to have a qualification which he or she does not actually possess.

A word may also have different CONNOTATIONS, which are the implied meanings and emotions a word evokes in the reader. For example, a cubicle is a simply a walled desk in an office, but for many the word implies a constrictive, uninspiring workplace. Connotations can vary greatly between cultures and even between individuals.

Lastly, authors might make use of FIGURATIVE LANGUAGE, which is the use of a word to imply something other than the word's literal definition. This is often done by comparing two things. If you say *I felt like a butterfly when I got a new haircut*, the listener knows you don't resemble an insect but instead felt beautiful and transformed.

Word Structure

Although you are not expected to know every word in the English language for the ACT, you can use deductive reasoning to determine the answer choice that is the best match for the word in question by breaking down unfamiliar vocabulary. Many complex words can be broken down into three main parts:

prefix – root – suffix

ROOTS are the building blocks of all words. Every word is either a root itself or has a root. Just as a plant cannot grow without roots, neither can vocabulary, because a word must have a root to give it meaning. The root is what is left when you strip away all the prefixes and suffixes from a word. For example, in the word *unclear*, if you take away the prefix *un–*, you have the root *clear*.

Roots are not always recognizable words; they generally come from Latin or Greek words like *nat*, a Latin root meaning *born*. The word *native*, which describes a person born in a referenced place, comes from this root, as does the word *prenatal*, meaning *before birth*. It's important to keep in mind, however, that roots do not always match the exact definitions of words, and they can have several different spellings.

PREFIXES are syllables added to the beginning of a word, and **SUFFIXES** are syllables added to the end of the word. Both carry assigned meanings and can be attached to a word to completely change the word's meaning or to enhance the word's original meaning.

Take the word *prefix* itself as an example: *fix* means to place something securely and *pre–* means before. Therefore, *prefix* means to place something before or in front of. Now let's look at a suffix: in the word *portable*, *port* is a root which means to move or carry. The suffix *-able* means that something is possible. Thus, *portable* describes something that can be moved or carried.

Although you cannot determine the meaning of a word by a prefix or suffix alone, you can use this knowledge to eliminate answer choices; understanding whether the word is positive or negative can give you the partial meaning of the word.

Comparing Passages

In addition to analyzing single passages, the ACT will also require you to compare two passages. Usually these passages will discuss the same topic, and it will be your task to identify the similarities and differences between the authors' main ideas, supporting details, and tones.

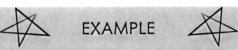
EXAMPLE

Read the two passages below and answer the following questions.

Passage One

Today, there is an epidemic of unhealthy children in the United States who will face health problems in adulthood due to poor diet and lack of exercise during their childhoods: in 2012, the Centers for Disease Control found that 18 percent of students aged 6-11 were obese. This is a problem for all Americans, as adults with chronic health issues are adding to the rising cost of healthcare. A child who grows up living an unhealthy lifestyle is likely to become an adult who does the same.

Because exercise is critical for healthy development in children, it is vital that school systems and parents encourage their children to engage in a minimum of thirty minutes of cardiovascular exercise each day. Even this small amount of exercise has been proven to decrease the likelihood that young people will develop diabetes, obesity, and other health issues as adults. In addition to exercise, children need a proper diet rich in fruits and vegetables so that they can grow and develop physically. Starting a good diet early also teaches children healthy eating habits they will carry into adulthood.

Passage Two

When was the last time you took a good, hard look at a school lunch? For many adults, it's probably been years—decades even—since they last thought about students' midday meals. If they did stop to ponder, they might picture something reasonably wholesome if not very exciting: a peanut butter and jelly sandwich paired with an apple, or a traditional plate of meat, potatoes and veggies. At worst, they may think, kids are making due with some pizza and a carton of milk.

The truth, though, is that many students aren't even getting the meager nutrients offered up by a simple slice of pizza. Instead, schools are serving up heaping helpings of previously frozen, recently fried delicacies like french fries and chicken nuggets. These high-carb, low-protein options are usually paired with a limp, flavorless, straight-from-the-freezer vegetable that quickly gets tossed in the trash. And that carton of milk? It's probably a sugar-filled chocolate sludge, or it's been replaced with a student's favorite high-calorie soda.

So what, you might ask. Kids like to eat junk food—it's a habit they'll grow out of soon enough. Besides, parents can always pack lunches for students looking for something better. But is that really the lesson we want to be teaching our kids? Many of those children aren't going to grow out of bad habits; they're going to reach adulthood thinking that ketchup is a vegetable. And students in low-income families are particularly impacted by the sad state of school food. These parents rely on schools to provide a warm, nutritious meal because they don't have the time or money to prepare food at home. Do we really want to be punishing these children with soggy meat patties and salt-soaked potato chips?

Both authors are arguing for the importance of improving childhood nutrition. How do the authors' strategies differ?

A) Passage 1 presents several competing viewpoints while Passage 2 offers a single argument.

B) Passage 1 uses scientific data while Passage 2 uses figurative language.

C) Passage 1 is descriptive while Passage 2 uses a cause-effect structure.

D) Passage 1 has a friendly tone while the tone of Passage 2 is angry.

The first author uses scientific facts (*the Centers for Disease Control found... and Even this small amount of exercise has been proven...*) to back up his argument, while the second uses figurative language (*the ironic delicacies and the metaphor sugar-filled chocolate sludge*), so the correct answer is B). Answer A) is incorrect because the first author does not present any opposing viewpoints. Answer C) is incorrect because Passage 2 does not have a cause-effect structure. And while the author of the second passage could be described as angry, the first author is not particularly friendly, so you can eliminate answer D) as well.

Both authors argue that

A) children should learn healthy eating habits at a young age.

B) low-income students are disproportionately affected by the low-quality food offered in schools.

C) teaching children about good nutrition will lower their chances of developing diabetes as adults.

D) schools should provide children an opportunity to exercise every day.

Both authors argue children should learn healthy eating habits at a young age (answer A). The author of Passage 1 states that a child who grows up living an unhealthy lifestyle is likely to become an adult who does the same, and the author of Passage 2 states that many of those children aren't going to grow out of bad habits—both of these sentences argue that it's necessary to teach children about nutrition early in life. Answers C) and D) are mentioned only by the author of Passage 1, and answer B) is only discussed in Passage 2.

Practice Problems

Descriptive Essay: Passage A is adapted from "How to Tell a Story" from the book How to Tell a Story *and Other Essays by Mark Twain (1835). Passage B is adapted from "Not That It Matters" from the book* The Pleasure of Writing *by A. A. Milne (1920).*

Passage A

I do not claim that I can tell a story as it ought to be told. I only claim to know how a story ought to be told, for I have been almost daily in the company of the most expert story-tellers for many years.

There are several kinds of stories, but only one difficult kind—the humorous. I will talk mainly about that one. The humorous story is American, the comic story is English, the witty story is French. The humorous story depends for its effect upon the manner of the telling; the comic story and the witty story upon the matter.

The humorous story may be spun out to great length, and may wander around as much as it pleases, and arrive nowhere in particular; but the comic and witty stories must be brief and end with a point. The humorous story bubbles gently along, the others burst.

The humorous story is strictly a work of art—high and delicate art—and only an artist can tell it; but no art is necessary in telling the comic and the witty story; anybody can do it. The art of telling a humorous story—understand, I mean by word of mouth, not print—was created in America, and has remained at home.

The humorous story is told gravely; the teller does his best to conceal the fact that he even dimly suspects that there is anything funny about it; but the teller of the comic story tells you beforehand that it is one of the funniest things he has ever heard, then tells it with eager delight, and is the first person to laugh when he gets through. And sometimes, if he has had good success, he is so glad and happy that he will repeat the "nub" of it and glance around from face to face, collecting applause, and then repeat it again. It is a pathetic thing to see.

Very often, of course, the rambling and disjointed humorous story finishes with a nub, point, snapper, or whatever you like to call it. Then the listener must be alert, for in many cases the teller will divert attention from that nub by dropping it in a carefully casual and indifferent way, with the pretence that he does not know it is a nub.

Artemus Ward used that trick a good deal; then when the belated audience presently caught the joke he would look up with innocent surprise, as if wondering what they had found to laugh at. Dan Setchell used it before him, Nye and Riley and others use it today.

But the teller of the comic story does not slur the nub; he shouts it at you—every time. And when he prints it, in England, France, Germany, and Italy, he italicizes it, puts some whooping exclamation-points after it, and sometimes explains it in a parenthesis. All of which is very depressing, and makes one want to renounce joking and lead a better life.

Passage B

Sometimes when the printer is waiting for an article which really should have been sent to him the day before, I sit at my desk and wonder if there is any possible subject in the whole world upon which I can possibly find anything to say. On one such occasion I left it to Fate, which decided, by means of a dictionary opened at random, that I should deliver myself of a few thoughts about goldfish.

(You will find this article later on in the book.) But to-day I do not need to bother about a subject. To-day I am without a care. Nothing less has happened than that I have a new nib in my pen.

In the ordinary way, when Shakespeare writes a tragedy, or Mr. Blank gives you one of his charming little essays, a certain amount of thought goes on before pen is put to paper. One cannot write "Scene I. An Open Place. Thunder and Lightning. Enter Three Witches," or "As I look up from my window, the nodding daffodils beckon to me to take the morning," one cannot give of one's best in this way on the spur of the moment. At least, others cannot. But when I have a new nib in my pen, then I can go straight from my breakfast to the blotting-paper, and a new sheet of foolscap fills itself magically with a stream of blue-black words. When poets and idiots talk of the pleasure of writing, they mean the pleasure of giving a piece of their minds to the public; with an old nib a tedious business. They do not mean (as I do) the pleasure of the artist in seeing beautifully shaped "k's" and sinuous "s's" grow beneath his steel. Anybody else writing this article might wonder "Will my readers like it?" I only tell myself "How the compositors will love it!"

Questions 1–3 refer to Passage B.

1. When the author writes *nothing less has happened in* to describe having a new nib in his pen, he means to convey that:

    F. a new nib in his pen is not very meaningful.

    G. a new nib in his pen is a rare and exciting event.

    H. a new nib being inserted in his pen is the last action he took.

    J. a new nib in his pen will make his writing better

2. Passage B indicates that compared to other writers, he is:

    A. similar, because he takes great pleasure in speaking his mind to an audience.

    B. similar, because he sometimes ignores publication deadlines.

    C. dissimilar, because he can write on any subject when he has to.

    D. dissimilar, because he takes pleasure in forming the letters over what they say.

3. Overall, which of the following best describes how the author feels about writing?

    F. It is a delicate activity subject to mood and environment.

    G. It is a scientific endeavor best approached methodically.

    H. It is a difficult and unpleasant task for many people.

    J. It is a hobby anyone can do successfully with the right equipment or supplies.

Questions 4–6 refer to Passage A.

4. What organizational method best describes how the author chooses to explain to the audience his ideas about humorous stories?

    A. The author describes the main features of a humorous story in order of importance in order to define it.

    B. The author describes the differences between a humorous story and a comic or witty story in order to clearly define a humorous story.

    C. The author gives an example of a good topic for a humorous story and describes how it should then be told.

    D. The author gives examples of famous tellers of humorous stories in order to explain how they tell one.

5. It is clear from the passage that the author would agree with which of the following statements?

    F. It is much more challenging to choose a good topic for a witty or comic story than to choose one for a humorous story.

    G. Humorous stories are common and easy to tell—one must simply find an appropriate topic.

    H. One who can tell a humorous story well deserves the respect and appreciation of other storytellers.

    J. The best humorous stories end with a nub because they combine the best components of both kinds of stories.

6. The author suggests that those who tell humorous stories are more skilled, while anyone at all can tell a comic story because:

    A. a humorous story depends in part upon the acting and speaking ability of the teller, while someone telling a comic story only needs to memorize the punch line.

    B. the storyteller has to make up a humorous story, but there are already many good comic stories in existence.

    C. only the storyteller thinks a comic or witty story is funny, which makes him or her seem pathetic; everyone laughs at a humorous story.

    D. a storyteller can laugh at his or her own humorous story without seeming pathetic, but this is not the case for a comic or witty story.

Questions 7–10 refer to both passages.

7. Which of the following best describes a topic addressed by both passages?

    A. The difficulty of the creative act

    B. The merits of a humorous story

    C. The difficulties of telling a story

    D. The skills of some famous writers

8. Which of the following is the best comparison of the tones in each passage?

    F. Passage A is respectful and admiring, and Passage B is faintly sarcastic

    G. Passage A is authoritative and direct, and Passage B is whimsical and amused.

    H. Both passages begin with uncertainty but end with a feeling of satisfied discovery.

    J. Both passages begin with contempt for other authors, but end with a sense of grudging respect for them.

9. Compared to the author of Passage B, the author of Passage A uses more

    A. analysis of specific examples of writing

    B. descriptions of writing

    C. comparisons between types of writing

    D. references to specific pieces of writing

10. Which of the following statements about writing and storytelling would both authors be likely to agree with?

    F. A good story should remain focused on a very specific topic or idea throughout.

    G. Writing a good story and telling a good story are similarly easy to accomplish.

    H. The best authors are those who plan their stories well in advance.

    J. Writing and telling stories are skills that require both skill and intuition.

Reading Answer Key

1.	G.	**6.**	A.
2.	D.	**7.**	A.
3.	F.	**8.**	G.
4.	B.	**9.**	C.
5.	H.	**10.**	J.

four

SCIENCE

40 questions ¦ 35 minutes

The Science section of the ACT is a little different from a typical science test: there won't be any questions that require you to recall science facts. You won't be asked *what is DNA*, for example, or be required to identify the parts of a cell. Instead, you'll have to interpret scientific passages. These passages might describe an experiment or present opposing viewpoints about a scientific issue; many of the passages will also include charts, tables, and figures. The questions that accompany each passage will ask about topics such as:

- ◆ interpreting data, tables, and figures
- ◆ predicting the outcome of an experiment
- ◆ finding similarities and differences in scientific arguments
- ◆ identifying the importance of an experimental outcome
- ◆ identifying supporting evidence for a scientific hypothesis or theory

While having a solid understanding of the life, physical, and earth sciences will help you on this section, specialized knowledge isn't required to answer the questions. When studying for the Science section, you're better off focusing on pacing and on reading strategies than on trying to relearn science facts.

The sections in this chapter provide a brief overview of scientific reasoning and data interpretation that will help you understand how to answer questions on the Science section. You can also prepare for Science by reviewing basic reading strategies. In fact, many of the skills you practiced for the Reading section will be vital here: you'll need to be able to pick out details from passages and identify the author's main argument. You'll also want to review the *Graphs and Charts* section from Chapter 2.

Pacing is often an issue on the Science section, so make sure to time yourself when taking practice tests.

Scientific Investigations

A theory and a hypothesis are both important aspects of science. There is a common misconception that they are one and the same, which is not true; however the two are very similar. A **HYPOTHESIS** is a proposed explanation for a phenomenon; it's usually based on observations or previous research. A **THEORY** is an explanation for a phenomenon that has been thoroughly tested and is generally accepted to be true by the scientific community.

Although science can never really "prove" something, it does provide a means to answering many questions about our natural world. Scientists use different types of investigations, each providing different types of results, based upon what they are trying to find. There are three main types of scientific investigations: descriptive, experimental, and comparative.

DESCRIPTIVE INVESTIGATIONS start with observations. A model is then constructed to provide a visual of what was seen: a description. Descriptive investigations do not generally require hypotheses, as they usually just attempt to find more information about a relatively unknown topic. **EXPERIMENTAL INVESTIGATIONS**, on the other hand, usually involve a hypothesis. These experiments are sometimes referred to as controlled experiments because they are performed in a controlled environment. During experimental investigations, all variables are controlled except for one: the dependent variable, which is part of the hypothesis being tested. Often, there are many tests involved in this process. Lastly, **COMPARATIVE INVESTIGATIONS** involve manipulating different groups in order to compare them with each other. There is no control during comparative investigations.

The Scientific Method

In order to ensure that experimental and comparative investigations are thorough and accurate, scientists use the scientific method, which has five main steps:

1. Observe and ask questions: look at the natural world to observe and ask questions about patterns and anomalies you see.
2. Gather information: look at what other scientists have done to see where your questions fit in with current research.
3. Construct a hypothesis: make a proposal that explains why or how something happens.

4. Experiment and test your hypothesis: set up an experimental investigation that allows you to test your hypothesis.

5. Analyze results and draw conclusions: examine your results and see whether they disprove your hypothesis. Note that you can't actually "prove" a hypothesis; you can only provide evidence to support it.

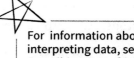

For information about interpreting data, see *Describing Sets of Data* in the Math chapter.

GO ON

Practice Problems

Atoms are made from protons, neutrons, and electrons. Every atom of a particular element has the same number of protons, but atoms of the same element may have different numbers of electrons and protons. An atom's atomic weight is defined as the sum of its protons and neutrons.

Isotopes are atoms of a particular element that have a different number of neutrons. Carbon-12, the most stable form of carbon atoms, has 6 protons and 6 neutrons. The 12 represents carbon-12's atomic weight: 6 + 6 = 12. Carbon-14, a common carbon isotope, has 6 protons and 8 neutrons.

Over time, isotopes undergo radioactive decay in which they lose protons, neutrons, or electrons in order to achieve a more stable ratio of particles. Carbon-14 atoms decay to nitrogen-14 at a predictable rate over time. In a process called carbon dating, scientists can use the percentage of carbon-14 remaining in a particular material to tell how old the material is.

Decay of Carbon-14

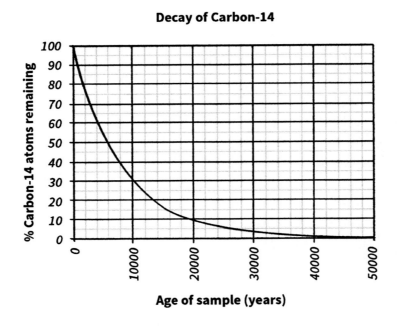

The graph above shows the rate of carbon-14 decay. The time it takes for half of the atoms in a sample to decay is called the element's half-life. After one half-life, the carbon-14 has decreased from 100% to 50%. During the second half-life, the carbon-14 decreases from 50% to 25%, and so on.

Other elemental isotopes can also be used to date samples. The following table shows the pattern of decay for potassium-40 (which decays to argon-40).

Table 4.1. Decay of Potassium-40

AGE OF SAMPLE (YEARS)	% POTASSIUM-40 ATOMS REMAINING
1.25 billion	50%
2.5 billion	25%
5 billion	6.5%
6.25 billion	3.25%

1. The half-life of carbon-14 is approximately

   A. 5,700 years

   B. 10,000 years

   C. 11,400 years

   D. 41,000 years

2. After 4 half-lives, what percentage of carbon-14 atoms remains?

   F. 50%

   G. 25%

   H. 12.5%

   J. 6.25%

3. During which of the following time periods does a material lose the greatest number of carbon-14 atoms?

   A. The first half-life

   B. The second half-life

   C. The third half-life

   D. None of the above; the material loses the same number of carbon-14 atoms during each half-life

4. How long does it take for the percent of carbon-14 atoms to reach zero?

   F. 30,000 years

   G. 40,000 years

   H. 6 half-lives

   J. The amount of carbon-14 never truly reaches zero, but it becomes undetectable after about 50,000 years.

5. What is the half-life of potassium-40?

   A. 625 million years

   B. 1.25 billion years

   C. 2.5 billion years

   D. 6.25 billion years

6. 5 billion years is equal to how many half-lives of potassium-40?

   F. 2

   G. 3

   H. 4

   J. 5

7. If a scientist wants to precisely date a fossil that he estimates must be at least 800 million years old, which of the following methods should he use?

   A. Measure the percentage of carbon-14 atoms remaining

   B. Measure the number of nitrogen-14 atoms present

   C. Measure the percentage of potassium-40 atoms remaining

   D. None of the above; the fossil is too old to date precisely

8. A geologist wants to estimate the age of a sample of sedimentary rock which is sandwiched between two layers of volcanic rock that were created by two separate volcanic eruptions. She determines that the bottom layer of volcanic rock has 30% of its original carbon-14 atoms remaining, and that the top layer has 40% remaining. What is her best estimate for the age of the sedimentary rock in between?

   F. 6,000-8,000 years old

   G. 8,000-10,000 years old

   H. 10,000-12,000 years old

   J. 6,000-10,000 years old

Science Answer Key

1.	A.	**5.**	B.
2.	J.	**6.**	H.
3.	A.	**7.**	C.
4.	J.	**8.**	G.

five

WRITING

1 prompt ¦ 40 minutes

The prompt on the Writing section will present a (slightly) controversial issue and several opposing viewpoints on that issue. You'll be asked to take a stand on the issue and write an essay that explains why you've taking that particular position. Your essay won't be graded on the particular position you take in your essay; instead, the graders will look at how well you develop and support your argument as well as the quality of the writing itself. A good essay will:

- have a clearly stated main idea
- demonstrate an understanding of multiple perspectives
- provide support for the main idea
- explore the implications of the stated position
- have a clear organization structure
- make use of varied sentence structure and transitions
- use appropriate language and tone

Structuring the Essay

There are a few different ways to organize an essay, but some basics apply no matter what the style.

Essays may differ in how they present an idea, but they all have the same basic parts—introduction, body, and conclusion. The most common essay types are persuasive essays and expository essays. A persuasive essay takes a position on an issue and attempts to show the reader why it is correct. An expository essay explains different aspects of an issue without necessarily taking a side.

Introductions

Present your argument or idea in the introduction. Usually, the introductory paragraph ends with a thesis statement, which clearly sets forth the position or point the essay will prove. The introduction is a good place to bring up complexities, counterarguments, and context, all of which will help the reader understand the reasoning behind your position on the issue at hand. Later, revisit those issues and wrap all of them up in the conclusion.

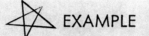 EXAMPLE

Below is an example of an introduction. Note that it provides some context for the argument, acknowledges an opposing perspective, and gives the reader a good idea of the issue's complexities. Pay attention to the thesis statement in the last few lines, which clearly states the author's position.

Technology has changed immensely in recent years, but today's generation barely notices—high school students are already experienced with the internet, computers, apps, cameras, cell phones, and more. Teenagers must learn to use these tools safely and responsibly. Opponents of 1:1 technology programs might argue that students will be distracted or misuse the technology, but that is exactly why schools must teach them to use it. By providing technology to students, schools can help them apply it positively by creating projects with other students, communicating with teachers and classmates, and conducting research for class projects. In a world where technology is improving and changing at a phenomenal rate, schools have a responsibility to teach students how to navigate that technology safely and effectively; providing each student with a laptop or tablet is one way to help them do that.

The Body Paragraphs

The body of an essay consists of a series of structured paragraphs. You may organize the body of your essay by creating paragraphs that describe or explain each reason you give in your thesis; addressing the issue as a problem and offering a solution in a separate paragraph; telling a story that demonstrates your point (make sure to break it into paragraphs around related ideas); or comparing and contrasting the merits of two opposing sides of the issue (make sure to draw a conclusion about which is better at the end).

Make sure that each paragraph is structurally consistent, beginning with a topic sentence to introduce the main idea, followed by supporting ideas and examples. No extra ideas unrelated to the paragraph's focus should appear. Use transition words and phrases to connect body paragraphs and improve the flow and readability of your essay.

In the *Providing Supporting Evidence* section you will find an example of a paragraph that is internally consistent and explains one of the main reasons given in the example introduction that you just read. Your essay should have one or more paragraphs like this to form the main body.

Conclusions

In order to end your essay smoothly, write a conclusion that reminds the reader why you were talking about these topics in the first place. Go back to the ideas in the introduction and thesis statement, but be careful not to simply restate your ideas; rather, reinforce your argument.

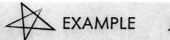 EXAMPLE

Here is a sample conclusion paragraph that could go with the introduction above. Notice that this conclusion talks about the same topics as the introduction (changing technology and the responsibility of schools), but it does not simply rewrite the thesis.

As technology continues to change, teens will need to adapt to it. Schools already teach young people myriad academic and life skills, so it makes sense that they would teach students how to use technology appropriately, too. Providing students with their own devices is one part of that important task, and schools should be supporting it.

Writing a Thesis Statement

The **THESIS**, or **THESIS STATEMENT**, is central to the structure and meaning of an essay. It presents the writer's argument, or position on an issue; in other words, it tells readers specifically what you think and what you will discuss. A strong, direct thesis statement is key to the organization of any essay. The thesis statement is typically located at the end of the introductory paragraph.

Writing a good thesis statement is as simple as stating your idea and why you think it is true or correct.

 EXAMPLE

The prompt:
Many high schools have begun to adopt 1:1 technology programs, meaning that each school provides every student with a computing device such as a laptop or tablet. Educators

who support these initiatives say that the technology allows for more dynamic collaboration and that students need to learn technology skills to compete in the job market. On the other hand, opponents cite increased distraction and the dangers of cyber-bullying or unsupervised internet use as reasons not to provide students with such devices.

In your essay, take a position on this question. You may write about either one of the two points of view given, or you may present a different point of view on this question. Use specific reasons and examples to support your position.

Possible thesis statements:

Providing technology to every student is good for education because it allows students to learn important skills such as typing, web design, and video editing; it also gives students more opportunities to work cooperatively with their classmates and teachers.

I disagree with the idea that schools should provide technology to students because most students will simply be distracted by the free access to games and websites when they should be studying or doing homework.

In a world where technology is improving and changing at a phenomenal rate, schools have a responsibility to teach students how to navigate that technology safely and effectively; providing each student with a laptop or tablet is one way to help them do that.

Providing Supporting Evidence

Your essay requires not only structured, organized paragraphs; it must also provide specific evidence supporting your arguments. Whenever you make a general statement, follow it with specific examples that will help to convince the reader that your argument has merit. These specific examples do not bring new ideas to the paragraph; rather, they explain or defend the general ideas that have already been stated.

The following are some examples of general statements and specific statements that provide more detailed support:

> **General**: Students may get distracted online or access harmful websites.

> **Specific**: Some students spend too much time using chat features or social media, or they get caught up in online games. Others spend time reading websites that have nothing to do with an assignment.

Specific: Teens often think they are hidden behind their computer screens. If teenagers give out personal information such as age or location on a website, it can lead to dangerous strangers seeking them out.

General: Schools can teach students how to use technology appropriately and expose them to new tools.

Specific: Schools can help students learn to use technology to work on class projects, communicate with classmates and teachers, and carry out research for classwork.

Specific: Providing students with laptops or tablets will allow them to get lots of practice using technology and programs at home, and only school districts can ensure that these tools are distributed widely, especially to students who may not have them at home.

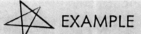 EXAMPLE

Below is an example of a structured paragraph that uses specific supporting ideas. This paragraph supports the thesis introduced above (see Introductions*).*

Providing students with their own laptop or tablet will allow them to explore new programs and software in class with teachers and classmates and to practice using it at home. In schools without laptops for students, classes have to visit computer labs where they share old computers that are often missing keys or that run so slowly they are hardly powered on before class ends. When a teacher tries to show students how to use a new tool or website, students must scramble to follow along and have no time to explore the new feature. If they can take laptops home instead, students can do things like practice editing video clips or photographs until they are perfect. They can email classmates or use shared files to collaborate even after school. If schools expect students to learn these skills, it is the schools' responsibility to provide students with enough opportunities to practice them.

This paragraph has some general statements:

> *… their own laptop or tablet will allow them to explore new programs and software… and to practice…*

> *…it is the schools' responsibility to provide… enough opportunities…*

It also has some specific examples to back them up:

…computers… run so slowly they are hardly powered on… students must scramble to follow along and have no time to explore…

They can email classmates or use shared files to collaborate…

Writing Well

Pay attention to the following details in order to ensure the clarity of your argument and to help readers understand the complexity and depth of your writing.

Transitions

Transitions are words, phrases, and ideas that help connect ideas throughout a text. You should use them between sentences and between paragraphs. Some common transitions include *then, next, in other words, as well, in addition to.* Be creative with your transitions, and make sure you understand what the transition you are using shows about the relationship between the ideas. For instance, the transition *although* implies that there is some contradiction between the first idea and the second.

Syntax

The way you write sentences is important to maintaining the reader's interest. Try to begin sentences differently. Make some sentences long and some sentences short. Write simple sentences. Write complex sentences that have complex ideas in them. Readers appreciate variety.

There are four basic types of sentences: simple, compound, complex, and compound-complex. Try to use some of each type. Be sure that your sentences make sense, though—it is better to have clear and simple writing that a reader can understand than to have complex, confusing syntax that does not clearly express the idea.

Word Choice and Tone

The words you choose influence the impression you make on readers. Use words that are specific, direct, and appropriate to the task. For instance, a formal text may benefit from complex sentences and impressive vocabulary, while it may be more appropriate to use simple vocabulary and sentences in writing intended for a young audience. Make use of strong vocabulary; avoid using vague, general words such as *good, bad, very,* or *a lot.* However, make sure that you are comfortable with the vocabulary you choose; if you are unsure about the word's meaning or its use in the context of your essay, don't use it at all.

Editing, Revising, and Proofreading

When writing a timed essay, you will not have very much time for these steps; spend any time you have left after writing the essay looking over it and checking for spelling and grammar mistakes that may interfere with a reader's understanding. Common mistakes to look out for include: subject/verb disagreement, pronoun/antecedent disagreement, comma splices and run-ons, and sentence fragments (phrases or dependent clauses unconnected to an independent clause).

Practice Problem

Read the passage and consider the following perspectives. Each suggests a particular way of thinking about the decision to require vaccination. Write an essay in which you evaluate multiple perspectives on the importance and consequence of required vaccination. In your essay, you should

◇ evaluate the perspectives given below

◇ explain your own position on the issue

◇ detail how your perspective compares to the others given

Vaccinations

Vaccines have been one of the most powerful and effective advances in modern medicine. Throughout most of our history, humans could do little to prevent the spread of disease. Now, we have the ability to create in most people an immunity to specific viruses and bacteria. Thanks to vaccines, diseases such as polio, malaria, and whooping cough have all but disappeared from the western world. Concerns about vaccines remain, however. Many people claim a religious objection to medical interference, while others worry about the safety of the young children being vaccinated. Scientists argue in return that allowing a few to opt out of vaccination endangers the whole community by allowing these diseases a foothold to return. Given that religious and bodily freedom are such an integral part of our culture, we must decide how to balance the safety of the community with the ability of citizens to make decisions about their own bodies and those of their children.

Perspective One

The ability to make medical decisions both for ourselves and our families is one of the most basic human rights. If we require a person to receive vaccinations against her will, we erode personal autonomy and freedom for everyone.

Perspective Two

A reasonable society should be able to balance the safety and right of its citizens. Exceptions should be made for those with reasonable objections to vaccination.

Perspective Three

People must give up a measure of personal autonomy in order to successfully live as part of society. The safety of the community is more important than any single person's right to refuse vaccination.

PART II: TEST YOUR KNOWLEDGE

six

ENGLISH PRACTICE TEST

In the following passages, there are numbered and underlined words and phrases that correspond with the questions in the right-hand column. You are to choose the answer that best completes the statement grammatically, stylistically, and/or logically. If you think the original version is best, select "NO CHANGE."

Passage I: Food trucks

Across the United States, a new trend in dining has taken (1)hold. Cities like Austin, Portland, San Francisco, and Seattle are seeing a significant increase in one particular type of dining establishment—the food truck. Though the modern food truck phenomenon is still in (2)it's prime, mobile dining is in no way

1. **A.** NO CHANGE
   B. hold in cities
   C. hold of cities
   D. hold, cities

2. **F.** NO CHANGE
   G. its
   H. its'
   J. it is

(3)a unique, novel idea: precursors to the modern food truck can be traced back as far as the 1800s.

3. **A.** NO CHANGE
   B. a new or novel idea
   C. a novel thought or idea
   D. a novel idea

The earliest predecessors to the modern food truck (4)was actually not trucks; in fact, they were not motorized at all.

(5)Push carts were some of the earliest vehicles for mobile food distribution and were popular in urban areas like New York City, where workers needed access to quick, cheap lunches.

(6)Instead, while these carts were mobile,

(7)they were not always available when they were most needed.

In the late 1800s, two new inventions marked important milestones in the development of the modern food truck. In 1866, Charles Goodnight created the first

(8)chuckwagon and a covered wagon that served as a mobile kitchen for cowmen who were herding cattle northward for sale. The cooks, or "cookies," who traveled with the cowmen

4. **F.** NO CHANGE
    G. were
    H. are
    J. is

5. **A.** NO CHANGE
    B. Push carts were some of the earliest vehicles for mobile food distribution, popular in urban areas where workers needed access to quick, cheap lunches like New York City.
    C. Popular in urban areas like New York City, some of the earliest vehicles for mobile food distribution were push carts, which were located wherever workers needed access to quick, cheap lunches.
    D. Some of the earliest vehicles were push carts for food distribution, popular in urban areas, like New York, where workers needed quick, cheap lunches in the city.

6. **F.** NO CHANGE
    G. However,
    H. As a result,
    J. Therefore,

7. Given that all of the choices are true, which of the following would be most effective in highlighting one of the major differences between the push cart and the modern food truck?
    A. NO CHANGE
    B. they sometimes stayed in one place for long periods of time.
    C. they were not equipped with the tools necessary to prepare the food.
    D. they often had the same people working in them all the time.

8. **F.** NO CHANGE
    G. chuckwagon, and a covered wagon
    H. chuckwagon, a covered wagon
    J. chuckwagon; a covered wagon

would wake early and prepare meals of beans, dried meats, and biscuits using the tools and ingredients on the chuckwagon. (9) Similarly, in 1872, a food vendor named Walter Scott conceived of the lunch wagon, from which he would serve sandwiches, coffee, and desserts to journalists outside a Providence, Rhode Island newspaper office.

[1] In the 1900s, mobile dining took even newer forms, as the invention of motorized transportation began to transform the industry. [2] Ice cream trucks followed in the 1950s, serving children and adults alike cold treats on hot summer afternoons. [3] In the 1960s, large food service trucks called "roach coaches" began to pop up near densely populated urban areas, <u>often serving cheap meals from grungy kitchens.</u> (10)

9. If the writer were to delete the preceding sentence, the paragraph would primarily lose:
   A. details about how cooks on the cattle trails came to be called "cookies."
   B. a transition between two points in the paragraph.
   C. details about how the cooks made food on the chuckwagons.
   D. information about the meaning of the phrase mobile kitchen.

10. The writer is considering deleting the words *cheap* and *grungy* from the preceding sentence. Should the writer make these deletions?
    F. Yes, because the words distract from the main idea of the sentence.
    G. Yes, because the words are offensive to people who like food trucks.
    H. No, because the words provide insight into the origin of the term "roach coach."
    J. No, because they provide more information about early food trucks.

GO ON

(11)

11. Upon reviewing the previous paragraph and realizing that some information had been left out, the writer composes the following sentence:

During the WWII era, mobile canteens popped up near Army bases to serve quick, easy meals to the troops.

The most logical placement for this sentence would be:

A. before sentence 1
B. before sentence 2
C. before sentence 3
D. after sentence 3

(12)In recent years, the food truck industry has transformed the mobile dining experience from one of convenience to one of excitement.

12. F. NO CHANGE
G. Consequently,
H. Therefore,
J. In conclusion,

Today, city dwellers and tourists (13)will have flocked to food trucks not only for ease and affordability, but also for unique foods, new flavors, and fun experiences. In some places, whole streets or even neighborhoods are devoted to hosting these food trucks, (14)so they are easier than ever to access.

13. A. NO CHANGE
B. are flocking
C. have flocked
D. have been flocking

14. Which of the following choices would provide an ending most consistent with the statement made in the first sentence of the paragraph?

F. NO CHANGE
G. so you rarely run out of delicious options.
H. but sometimes these areas can be busy.
J. and people travel from all over the city, sometimes even farther, to try what they're offering.

(15)

Question 15 asks about the preceding passage as a whole.

15. Suppose the writer had intended to write an essay on the historical development of the modern food truck. Would this essay successfully fulfill that goal?

   A. Yes, because it provides detailed information about the inventor who designed the first food truck.

   B. Yes, because it provides a brief overview of the trends and innovations that preceded the modern food truck.

   C. No, because it is primarily a descriptive essay about the modern food truck trend and its followers.

   D. No, because it focuses primarily on the differences between modern food trucks and older forms of mobile food distribution.

Passage II: Neil deGrasse Tyson

Most people struggle to find what they want to do with their (16)lives; but Neil deGrasse Tyson knew when he was 9 years old.

16. **F.** NO CHANGE
   G. lives, however,
   H. lives,
   J. lives, but

(17)While visiting the Hayden Planetarium in New York City for the first time, Tyson discovered that he was fascinated by outer space. From that moment on, he pursued his interest wholeheartedly and ultimately came to be one of the (18)more famous and important astrophysicists of our day: his career has undoubtedly shaped the public's thinking

17. **A.** NO CHANGE
   B. Because of his visiting
   C. Having visited
   D. He visited

18. **F.** NO CHANGE
   G. most famous
   H. more highly famous
   J. famous

GO ON

(19)about space and space exploration.

Since the beginning of his professional career, Tyson has served on a number of

important commissions and (20)councils, and have shaped the way the government and its agencies approach space exploration. Two commissions to which he was appointed by President George W. Bush served to guide the future of American space research and travel by influencing policy and (21)agenda formation, a third appointment,

(22)to NASA's esteemed Advisory Council— allowed Tyson to contribute to deliberations on NASA's financial planning. In all, Tyson had a great deal of political clout when it came to discussions of America's future in space.

[1] Still, Tyson's political influence is often outshined by his popular influence. [2] On top of his professional accomplishments, he has found fame by making astronomy not only interesting (23)but nevertheless accessible to the average citizen. [3] In addition to writing a number of books for public consumption, Tyson has produced and hosted numerous popular documentaries and documentary series about space.

19. Which of the following alternatives to the underlined portion would NOT be acceptable?
   A. on space
   B. when it comes to space
   C. in space
   D. regarding space

20. F. NO CHANGE
   G. councils; which
   H. councils, these
   J. councils, which

21. A. NO CHANGE
   B. agenda formation. A third
   C. agenda formation, then, a third
   D. agenda formation; and a third

22. F. NO CHANGE
   G. to NASA's esteemed Advisory Council
   H. to NASA's Advisory Council;
   J. to NASA's esteemed Advisory Council,

23. A. NO CHANGE
   B. and still
   C. but also
   D. but still

(24)

[4] (25)Furthermore, Tyson's radio show and podcast, called *StarTalk Radio*, combines science, comedy, and celebrity guests to appeal to a diverse following.

(26) [5] Over the course of his career, Tyson has also earned a plethora of awards and acknowledgments for his unrelenting efforts at making space a bigger focus of public discourse. [6] NASA awarded him the highest honor it

(27)awards to citizens, the NASA Distinguished Public Service Medal, and the International Astronomical Union named an asteroid, 13123

24. The writer is considering adding the following phrase to the preceding sentence, following a comma:

including Cosmos: A SpaceTime Odyssey, a series that was nominated for thirteen Emmy awards.

Should the writer add this sentence here?

F. Yes, because it adds relevant information about the popularity of Tyson's documentary series.

G. Yes, because it is unusual for an astrophysicist to win Emmy awards.

H. No, because the show did not win any of the awards.

J. No, because Tyson is an astrophysicist and not an entertainer.

25. Which of the following alternatives to the underlined portion would be LEAST acceptable?

A. Additionally,

B. Moreover,

C. Also,

D. On the other hand,

26. If the writer were to delete the phrase *to appeal to a diverse following* from the preceding sentence, the paragraph would primarily lose:

F. details about how Tyson chooses his celebrity guests.

G. information about the mission of Tyson's radio show.

H. a description of what listeners can expect on Tyson's radio show.

J. nothing at all because it is not relevant information.

27. A. NO CHANGE

B. awards to citizen's

C. awards to citizens'

D. awards' to citizens

GO ON

Tyson, in his honor. (28)

Today, Neil deGrasse Tyson works as the Director of the Hayden Planetarium in New York City, the same planetarium where

(29)he first discovered his love of astronomy. Through his work at the planetarium, he continues to pursue his mission of making astronomy and space exploration more

(30)accessible to the general public.

28. The writer has decided to divide the preceding paragraph into two. The best place to add the paragaph break would be:

   F. after sentence 3, because the topic shifts from Tyson's film and television experience to his work on a radio show.

   G. after sentence 2, because it would indicate that the writer is going to discuss more detail about Tyson's accomplishments.

   H. after sentence 4, because it signals a shift from a discussion of Tyson's work to a section about his honors and acknowledgments.

   J. nowhere. The paragraph should not be divided.

29. Given that all of the following are true, which choice would best tie back to the beginning of the essay and explain why the job at the planetarium might be meaningful to Neil deGrasse Tyson?

   A. NO CHANGE

   B. he continues to conduct research.

   C. he works long hours almost every night.

   D. he hopes to work until he retires.

30. Which of the following options would best reinforce the tone and main idea of the essay?

   F. NO CHANGE

   G. interesting to us regular folk.

   H. important to policy makers.

   J. simple for young scientists.

Passage III: Immigration
[1]

(31)<u>As a young child, my family moved all the around the world following my dad's job.</u> Usually, we would live in each new country for about a year, during which time I

(32)<u>had attended</u> an international school. Like us, most of the

(33)<u>family's whose students</u> attended these international schools were immigrants, people who

(34)<u>had moved</u> to the country from other countries. At one of my first international schools, when I was eight years old, my teacher taught a lesson about the word *immigration*. She told us that it comes from the word *migrate*, which means to move to and settle in (35)<u>a new location</u>, either temporarily or permanently.

31. **A.** NO CHANGE
    B. My family moved all around the world when I was a young child for my dad's job.
    C. My dad's job caused my family to move all around the world as a young child.
    D. When I was a young child, my family moved all around the world following my dad's job.

32. **F.** NO CHANGE
    G. would attend
    H. have attended
    J. will attend

33. **A.** NO CHANGE
    B. families who's students
    C. families whose students
    D. family's whose students'

34. **F.** NO CHANGE
    G. have moved
    H. moving
    J. will have moved

35. **A.** NO CHANGE
    B. a new and different location
    C. a different location where they would live
    D. a new location with different surroundings

GO ON

[2]

As I got older, I learned that many animals migrate (36)as well; and fish, birds, mammals, reptiles, amphibians, and even insects will move to new locations in search of more hospitable conditions. Most animal migration is (37)cyclical and occurs at predictable times each year in response to seasonal changes. This type of migration occurs, for instance, when geese fly south to stay warm during the cold, inhospitable winter months and then return north during the

summer when the weather is mild. (38)

[3]

One of the largest and most stunning examples of cyclical migration occurs in Africa's Serengeti National Park. This mass migration occurs over the course of a full year, during which time more than two million

(39)animals including wildebeests, zebras, and gazelles, move around the outskirts of the park in search of food, water, and a safe place to bear their children.

36. **F.** NO CHANGE
    G. as well. Fish
    H. as well, fish
    J. as well, for example, fish

37. Which of the following alternatives to the underlined portion would be LEAST acceptable?
    A. cyclical in that it occurs
    B. cyclical, being that it occurs
    C. cyclical, meaning that it occurs
    D. cyclical, occuring

38. The writer is considering deleting the preceding sentence from the essay. The sentence should NOT be deleted because:
    F. it is important that the reader be able to name at least one species that completes a cyclical migration.
    G. it describes how some animals do not have a permanent home.
    H. it gives the reader information about how to avoid extreme temperatures.
    J. it provides a simple, illustrative example of how seasonal changes can drive animal behavior.

39. **A.** NO CHANGE
    B. animals, including wildebeests, zebras, and gazelles
    C. animals, including wildebeests, zebras, and gazelles,
    D. animals, including wildebeests zebras, and gazelles,

(40) Thus, like almost all instances of cyclical migration, the mass migration of animals in Serengeti National Park occurs predictably in response to natural weather and water cycles.

[4]

(41)Consequently, sometimes animals must migrate for a specific reason in unique circumstances. For example, overpopulation in a concentrated area could lead to famine, causing portions of the population to move elsewhere in search of alternative food sources. Likewise, natural phenomenon like wildfires or volcano eruptions might make an area uninhabitable and force out the animals who were living there.

[5]

Human migration, like my family's trek around the world, most often occurs in this (42)irregular form. Some jobs or family situations might require regular, predictable movements between locations, but, like us, most people move with the knowledge that they will not be returning to the place they just left. Instead, they know that they

40. At this point in the paragraph, the writer is considering adding the following sentence:

Along the way, they must contend with dangerous temperatures, extreme exhaustion, and threatening predators.

Should the writer make this addition here?

F. Yes, because it provides relevant information about why some animals do not survive migration.

G. Yes, because it gives the reader details about how migrations can influence the size of a population.

H. No, because it misleads the reader about the purpose of migration.

J. No, because it distracts from the main point of the paragraph.

41. Which of the following options provides the most effective transition for introducing the second kind of (irregular) migration?

A. NO CHANGE

B. On the other hand,

C. Nevertheless,

D. Unfortunately,

42. Which of the following alternatives to the underlined word would be LEAST acceptable?

F. aimless

G. intermittent

H. erratic

J. sporadic

GO ON

will soon be settling down to start a new life in

a new home—(43)even if it's just for a year.

(44)

(45)

43. Which of the following options most effectively ties the subject of migration back to the narrator's personal experience?

   A. NO CHANGE

   B. and hopefully they will be happy.

   C. though sometimes it doesn't work out.

   D. no matter what their reason is for moving.

Questions 44 and 45 ask about the preceding passage as a whole.

44. For the sake of logic and coherence, Paragraph 5 should be placed:

   F. where it is now.

   G. before paragraph 1.

   H. after paragraph 1.

   J. after paragraph 2.

45. Suppose the writer had intended to write a brief essay explaining a behavior that humans and animals share. Would this essay successfully fulfill that goal?

   A. Yes, because it gives the reader insight into how humans and animals can learn to coexist in different climates.

   B. Yes, because it provides information about the migration behaviors of both humans and animals.

   C. No, because it focuses on his own family's migration around the world.

   D. No, because it fails to provide relevant information about animal families.

Passage IV

The Grand Canyon is a landmark (46)who's enormity cannot truly be understood until it is experienced. The canyon, which was formed by millions of years of erosion by the Colorado River, is over one mile deep, nearly twenty miles wide, and over two hundred fifty feet long. It is located in northern Arizona and falls primarily inside Grand Canyon National Park, which (47)bisects the Kaibab National Forest. Adjacent to the park

(48)is three Indian reservations—the Hualapai,

the Kaibab Paiute, and the Navajo. (49)

Management of this enormous landmark is achieved through the cooperation of many different groups. The tribal nations that

46. **F.** NO CHANGE
    G. of which its
    H. where
    J. whose

47. Which of the following alternatives to the underlined portion would be LEAST acceptable?
    A. separates
    B. crosses
    C. intersects
    D. cuts across

48. **F.** NO CHANGE
    G. are
    H. were
    J. exists

49. The writer is considering deleting the following phrase from the preceding sentence, ending the sentence with a period after the word *reservations*:

    the Hualapai, the Kaibab Paiute, and the Navajo

    If the writer were to make this deletion, the paragraph would primarily lose:
    A. information about the background of the Native American people who work in the canyon.
    B. details about control over the land surrounding the Grand Canyon.
    C. insight into the history of the Grand Canyon.
    D. nothing because the information is irrelevant.

GO ON

(50)would reside in the area work alongside governmental

50. F. NO CHANGE
    G. had resided
    H. are residing
    J. reside

(51)organizations, like the National Park Service to ensure that the lands are protected and tourists are kept

51. A. NO CHANGE
    B. organizations—like the National Park service,
    C. organizations, like the National Park Service,
    D. organizations like the National Park Service,

(52)safe and free from harm.

52. F. NO CHANGE
    G. safe.
    H. safe and out of harm's way.
    J. safe and avoid injury.

[1](53)Consequently, the Grand Canyon is one of the most popular tourist attractions in the world, drawing upwards of five million

visitors every year. (54)

53. A. NO CHANGE
    B. In fact,
    C. Nevertheless,
    D. Therefore,

[2] People come from all over the world to see the massive landmark, so activities and attractions are abundant. [3] Outdoor activities

54. Given that all of the following choices are true, which would most effectively support the claim made earlier in the sentence?
    F. NO CHANGE
    G. even though most of its visitors don't stay long.
    H. though it is still surpassed in popularity by the Eiffel Tower.
    J. making its upkeep a difficult job.

(55)like hiking, rafting, and camping, are popular, especially during the cooler months of spring and autumn. [4] Other activities like

55. A. NO CHANGE
    B. like, hiking, rafting, and camping
    C. like, hiking, rafting and camping,
    D. like hiking, rafting, and camping

airplane and helicopter flyovers allow visitors a
(56)broader perspective of the canyon.

(57)

(58)Most activities at the Grand Canyon, however, are extremely limited by the weather, which varies significantly based on season and time of day. During the summer months, temperatures inside the canyon can reach above one hundred degrees

(59)Fahrenheit; during winter months, the temperature can drop below zero degrees. Even daytime and nighttime temperatures can vary substantially,

56. Which of the following is the best placement for the underlined word?

   F. where it is now

   G. after the word *like*

   H. after the word *allow*

   J. before the word *canyon*

57. The writer is considering adding the following true statement to the preceding paragraph:

   Visitors can even walk over and look down at the canyon from the Grand Canyon SkyWalk, a transparent bridge that juts out in a horseshoe shape from one side of the canyon.

   This sentence would most logically be placed after:

   A. sentence 1

   B. sentence 2

   C. sentence 3

   D. sentence 4

58. **F.** NO CHANGE

   G. Being extremely limited by the weather, most activities at the Grand Canyon vary significantly based on season and time of day.

   H. Most activities at the Grand Canyon are extremely limited by the weather and based on the season and time of day.

   J. Based on the season and time of day, the weather has an extremely limiting effect on activities at the Grand Canyon.

59. Which of the following alternatives to the underlined portion would NOT be acceptable?

   A. Fahrenheit, and during

   B. Fahrenheit, during

   C. Fahrenheit, whereas during

   D. Fahrenheit, but during

GO ON

(60)so it is important for visitors to follow weather forecasts and pack carefully.

60. Which of the following would provide the most relevant ending to this essay by offering advice to the reader about how to prepare for a trip to the canyon?
  F. NO CHANGE
  G. but the changes are manageable if you're prepared.
  H. and visitors are often surprised by the drastic variation.
  J. and it is impossible to predict what the weather will look like on any given day.

Passage V: Hot French Bread

When I was seventeen years old, I applied for jobs for the first time in my life. A few days after submitting my application at the local bakery, (61)the manager called to offer me an interview for the position of bakery clerk. I

61. A. NO CHANGE
  B. I received a call from the manager, who offered me an interview for the position of bakery clerk.
  C. an interview for the position of bakery clerk was offered to me.
  D. the manager, offering me an interview for the position of bakery clerk, called me.

gladly accepted the offer and (62) set up a time to meet with her. Just a week after that, I found myself standing behind the counter at my new place of employment.

62. F. NO CHANGE
  G. am setting up
  H. would set up
  J. will set up

My job at the bakery (63)is an arduous one, but I enjoyed every moment of it. Every day when I walked in, I would be greeted by an array of wonderful smells—cookies, cakes, and hot, fresh bread. Immediately, I would

63. A. NO CHANGE
  B. was
  C. were
  D. are

(64)put on my apron, tying up my long hair, and getting to work icing and packaging the delicious creations that Eduardo—the baker—had just pulled out of the oven. Most days I packed cookies,

(65)but it wasn't the only thing I did. On more exciting days, I iced cupcakes with colorful buttercream frosting and packed them into neat containers.

(66)

64. **F.** NO CHANGE
G. putting on my apron, tie up my long hair, and get to work icing and packaging
H. put on my apron, tie up my long hair, and getting to work icing and packaging
J. put on my apron, tie up my long hair, and get to work icing and packaging

65. Given that all of the following options are true, which provides the strongest support for the claim, made in the first sentence of the paragraph, about the arduousness of the job?
A. NO CHANGE
B. often as many as two thousand of them in one day.
C. and those days were the easiest.
D. which always made me want cookies so badly.

66. The writer is considering deleting the phrase *with colorful buttercream frosting* from the preceding sentence. If this phrase were deleted, the paragraph would primarily lose:
F. details that support the narrator's claim that icing cupcakes could make a day more exciting.
G. important information about the type of job the narrator was doing.
H. relevant information about what kinds of sweets the bakery was selling.
J. details about what the narrator had to do before packaging the cupcakes.

(67)

    In addition to packaging the baked goods,

<u>(68)I was responsible for ensuring that customer service at the bakery was top-notch.</u> I helped

<u>(69)them</u> find items when they couldn't, and I sliced

<u>(70)there</u> loaves of bread according to the slice thickness they chose. I even wrote messages on the cakes as requested,

67. The writer is considering adding the following sentence to the preceding paragraph:

    Regardless of what I was packaging, Eduardo almost always tried to make at least one extra so that I would have a treat to munch on while I worked.

    Should this addition be made?

    A. Yes, because it is important for the reader to know that the narrator and Eduardo were friends.

    B. Yes, because it provides additional insight into why the narrator liked the job of bakery clerk.

    C. No, because it distracts from the main point of the paragraph.

    D. No, because the narrator's friendship with Eduardo was more significant than free sweets.

68. **F.** NO CHANGE

    G. Taking care of customer needs was also my responsibility.

    H. Customers also approached me with questions and requests.

    J. The responsibility of taking care of the customers was also mine.

69. **A.** NO CHANGE

    B. it

    C. shoppers

    D. they

70. **F.** NO CHANGE

    G. their

    H. some

    J. they're

(71)especially when a customer was choosing a cake for a birthday.

Still, my favorite part of every day at the bakery did not involve icing or free sample cookies. Rather, my favorite part of every day was 3 p.m., when it was time to take the hot, fresh French bread out of the oven. At 3 p.m. exactly, the oven timer would beep, and I would slip on the giant oven mitts. Then, after opening the monstrous (72)oven door; I would slide out the bread trays and move each loaf carefully into a

(73)long brown paper bag. Finally, I would push my basket of fresh bread out into the store and yell, "hot French bread!" In no time, customers from all corners of the store would make their way to the bakery for their fresh loaves of bread. My job at the bakery was not an easy one, (74)but I enjoyed knowing that our customers were leaving the store with smiles on their faces and warm, fresh bread in their bags.

71. Given that all of the following choices are true, which would demonstrate the amount of skill the narrator had to have in order to write on cakes?
  A. NO CHANGE
  B. always allowing the customer to choose the color.
  C. occasionally making mistakes and having to correct them with more icing.
  D. careful not to make a mess of the beautiful iced decorations that were already there.

72. F. NO CHANGE
  G. oven door, then I would
  H. oven door, I would
  J. oven door—I would

73. A. NO CHANGE
  B. long, brown paper bag
  C. long brown, paper bag
  D. long, brown paper, bag

74. Given that all of the following options are true, which most effectively supports the statement made in the first sentence of the second paragraph?
  F. NO CHANGE
  G. but the pay was worth it, and the free sweets were delicious.
  H. so I got a good amount of exercise while I was there.
  J. but I stayed for three full years because it was a good opportunity to build my résumé.

GO ON

75. Suppose the writer had intended to write an essay about the first week at a new job. Would this essay fulfill that goal?

A. Yes, because it provides information about how the narrator got the job in the first place.

B. Yes, because it discusses most of the responsibilities associated with being a bakery clerk.

C. No, because it focuses on the narrator's overall experience at the bakery rather than only the experience of the first week.

D. No, because it does not mention the narrator's prior experience.

Answer Key: English

1.	A.	26.	G.	51.	C.
2.	G.	27.	A.	52.	G.
3.	D.	28.	H.	53.	B.
4.	G.	29.	A.	54.	F.
5.	A.	30.	F.	55.	D.
6.	G.	31.	D.	56.	F.
7.	C.	32.	G.	57.	D.
8.	H.	33.	C.	58.	F.
9.	D.	34.	F.	59.	B.
10.	H.	35.	A.	60.	F.
11.	B.	36.	G.	61.	B.
12.	F.	37.	B.	62.	F.
13.	B.	38.	J.	63.	B.
14.	J.	39.	C.	64.	J.
15.	B.	40.	J.	65.	B.
16.	J.	41.	B.	66.	F.
17.	A.	42.	F.	67.	B.
18.	G.	43.	A.	68.	F.
19.	C.	44.	F.	69.	C.
20.	J.	45.	B.	70.	G.
21.	B.	46.	J.	71.	D.
22.	J.	47.	A.	72.	H.
23.	C.	48.	G.	73.	B.
24.	F.	49.	B.	74.	F.
25.	D.	50.	J.	75.	C.

seven

MATHEMATICS PRACTICE TEST

1. If $f(x) = 0.5^x + 1$, evaluate $f(-2)$.

    A. 0.75

    B. 1.25

    C. 2

    D. 4

    E. 5

2. Which expression is equivalent to $9x^2 + 21xy + 49y^2$?

    F. $(3x - 7y)^2$

    G. $(3x + 7y)^2$

    H. $(3x + 7)(x + y)$

    J. $(3x + 7y)(3x - 7)$

    K. $(3x + 7y)(3x - 7y)$

3. A material's specific heat capacity is the amount of energy needed to increase the temperature of 1 gram of that material by 1 degree Celsius. If the specific heat capacity of aluminum is $0.900 \frac{J}{(g \times °C)}$, how many joules of energy does it take to increase the temperature of 2 grams of aluminum by 4 degrees Celsius?

    A. 0.1 joules

    B. 3.6 joules

    C. 5.6 joules

    D. 7.2 joules

    E. 9.0 joules

4. Which of the following is an irrational number?

    F. -5

    G. $\frac{\pi}{2}$

    H. 1.085

    J. $\frac{9}{5}$

    K. 16

5. Some of a hotel's 200 rooms have 2 full beds and the rest have 1 queen bed. If the probability of getting a room with 2 full beds is 65%, how many rooms have 1 queen bed?

    A. 50 rooms

    B. 70 rooms

    C. 130 rooms

    D. 135 rooms

    E. 175 rooms

6. Mike leans a ladder against his house. If the ladder makes a 20 degree angle with the wall of the house, and the wall of the house makes a 90 degree angle with the ground, what angle does the ladder make with the ground?

    F. 20 degrees

    G. 60 degrees

    H. 70 degrees

    J. 90 degrees

    K. 120 degrees

7. Rafael and Marco are repainting their garage. If Rafael can paint $\frac{1}{6}$ of the garage in 20 minutes, and Marco can paint $\frac{1}{5}$ of the garage in 30 minutes, how long will it take them to paint the entire garage if they work together?

   A.   0 hour, 18 minutes

   B.   0 hour, 54 minutes

   C.   1 hour, 6.7 minutes

   D.   2 hour, 43.6 minutes

   E.   6 hour, 12 minutes

8. Simplify: $\begin{bmatrix} 2 & -3 & 12 \\ 10 & 1 & -8 \end{bmatrix} + \begin{bmatrix} 6 & 7 & -9 \\ -1 & 3 & 5 \end{bmatrix}$

   F. $\begin{bmatrix} 8 & 4 & 3 \\ 9 & 4 & -3 \end{bmatrix}$

   G. $\begin{bmatrix} 8 & 10 & 3 \\ 11 & 4 & 3 \end{bmatrix}$

   H. $\begin{bmatrix} 16 & -21 & -108 \\ -10 & 3 & -40 \end{bmatrix}$

   J. $\begin{bmatrix} 20 & 2 & 4 \\ 5 & 10 & 4 \end{bmatrix}$

   K. $\begin{bmatrix} 12 & -21 & 108 \\ -10 & 3 & -40 \end{bmatrix}$

9. Find the common ratio for a geometric sequence with terms $a_1 = -2$ and $a_6 = 486$.

   A.   −243

   B.   −6

   C.   −3

   D.   −2.5

   E.   40.5

10. Solve for x: $4x^2 - 2x > 6$

   F. $-3 < x < 2$

   G. $-2 < x < 3$

   H. $-1 < x < 1.5$

   J. $x < -2, x > 3$

   K. $x < -1, x > 1.5$

11. A bag contains twice as many red marbles as blue marbles, and the number of blue marbles is 88% of the number of green marbles. If g represents the number of green marbles, which of the following expressions represents the total number of marbles in the bag?

   A.   2.32g

   B.   2.64g

   C.   3.32g

   D.   3.64g

   E.   3.88g

12. Angie purchases a pair of running shoes on clearance for $65.00. If the shoes originally cost $85.00, what was her total discount?

   F.   23.5%

   G.   25.6%

   H.   39.2%

   J.   46.5%

   K.   53.5%

13. Ashley has been training for a 10 kilometer race. Her average training pace is 8 minutes and 15 seconds per mile. If she maintains this pace during the race, what will be her finishing time? (1 mile = 5280 feet; 1 foot = 0.3048 meters)

   A.   50 minutes, 53 seconds

   B.   51 minutes, 16 seconds

   C.   51 minutes, 23 seconds

   D.   82 minutes, 30 seconds

   E.   82 minutes, 42 seconds

14. Evaluate the expression $|3x - y| + |2y - x|$ if $x = -4$ and $y = -1$.

   F.   −13

   G.   −11

   H.   −6

   J.   11

   K.   13

15. If l_1 is perpendicular to l_2, and the equation of l_1 is $y = 2.5x - 3$, what is the slope of the line l_2?

   A. −2.5

   B. −0.4

   C. 0

   D. 0.33

   E. 0.4

16. A plane makes a trip of 246 miles. For some amount of time, the plane's speed is 115 miles per hour. For the remainder of the trip, the plane's speed is 250 miles per hour. If the total trip time is 72 minutes, how long did the plane fly at 115 miles per hour?

   F. 18 minutes

   G. 23 minutes

   H. 24 minutes

   J. 34 minutes

   K. 37 minutes

17. The volume, V, of a cylinder with radius r and height h can be found using the formula $V = \pi r^2 h$. If a cylindrical canister is 9 inches high and has a diameter of 5 inches, what is the maximum volume this canister can hold?

   A. 45 in²

   B. 141.4 in²

   C. 176.7 in²

   D. 317.93 in²

   E. 706.5 in²

18. Solve for x: $8(x + 5) = -3x - 48$

   F. $x = -8$

   G. $x = -0.625$

   H. $x = 0.625$

   J. $x = 8$

   K. $x = 12.8$

19. Find all possible values of x that satisfy the following equations: $16 - x \le 7x$ and $2x - 40 < 6$

   A. $2 < x \le 23$

   B. $2 \le x < 23$

   C. $2 \le x < 2\frac{2}{3}$

   D. $2\frac{2}{3} < x \le 23$

   E. $2\frac{2}{3} \le x < 23$

20. The volume, V, of a cone with radius r and height h can be found using the formula $V = \pi r^2 \frac{h}{3}$. A particular hourglass is made from 2 cones. The diameter of the base of each cone is 3 centimeters, and the height of the 2 cones combined is 12 centimeters. If the hourglass holds 4 cubic centimeters of sand, how much empty space remains inside the hourglass?

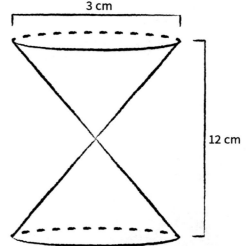

3 cm

12 cm

   F. 0.23 cm³

   G. 0.5 cm³

   H. 4.5 cm³

   J. 5 cm³

   K. 24.3 cm³

21. Right triangle $\triangle ABC$ has leg $\overline{AB} = 12$ inches. If angle $\angle BAC = 35°$, find hypotenuse $\overline{AC}$.

   A. 9.8 inches

   B. 12.0 inches

   C. 14.6 inches

   D. 17.1 inches

   E. 20.9 inches

22. A data set contains n points with a mean of μ. If a new data point with the value x is included in the data set, which of the following expressions is equal to the new mean?

F. $\frac{(\mu n + x)}{(n + 1)}$

G. $\frac{(\mu + x)}{n}$

H. $\frac{(\mu n + x)}{n}$

J. $\frac{(\mu + x)n}{(n + 1)}$

K. $\frac{\mu x n}{(n + 1)}$

23. Melissa is ordering fencing to enclose a square area of 5625 square feet. How many feet of fencing does she need?

A. 75 feet

B. 150 feet

C. 300 feet

D. 5625 feet

E. 11,250 feet

24. If $f(x) = x^2 + 3$ and $g(x) = 3x - 12$, then $f(g(5)) =$

F. 3

G. 12

H. 28

J. 72

K. 144

25. A pizza has a diameter of 10 inches. If you cut a slice with a central angle of 40°, what will be the surface area of the pizza slice?

A. 3.5 in²

B. 8.7 in²

C. 9.0 in²

D. 9.2 in²

E. 17.4 in²

26. Points B and C are on a circle, and a chord is formed by line segment $\overline{BC}$. If the distance from the center of the circle to point B is 10 centimeters, and the distance from the center of the circle to line segment $\overline{BC}$ is 8 centimeters, what is the length of line segment $\overline{BC}$?

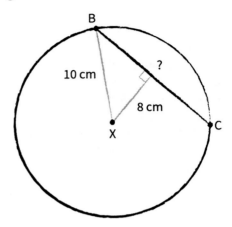

F. 4 centimeters

G. 6 centimeters

H. 12 centimeters

J. 14 centimeters

K. 18 centimeters

27. If $A = [-5 \quad 2 \quad 4]$ and $B = \begin{bmatrix} 0 & -3 \\ 10 & -6 \\ 7 & -1 \end{bmatrix}$, what is AB?

A. $[48 \quad -1]$

B. $[40 \quad 0]$

C. $\begin{bmatrix} 15 \\ 8 \\ 24 \end{bmatrix}$

D. $[85 \quad 34 \quad 68]$

E. The matrices cannot be multiplied.

28. In a particular raffle, a single ticket will be randomly drawn from a bag containing all the purchased tickets. If someone who buys 2 tickets has a 0.4% chance of winning, how many tickets were bought in total?

F. 8 tickets

G. 25 tickets

H. 50 tickets

J. 250 tickets

K. 500 tickets

29. Consider the equations $|3x - 5| = 23$ and $|10 + 4y| = 12$. If x and y are both negative numbers, what is $|y - x|$?

- **A.** 0.5
- **B.** 4.0
- **C.** 7.3
- **D.** 8.0
- **E.** 9.2

30. If $f(x) = 3^x - 2$, evaluate $f(5)$.

- **F.** 13
- **G.** 27
- **H.** 123
- **J.** 241
- **K.** 243

31. Solve for x: $16x^2 + 8x + 1 = 0$

- **A.** $x = -4, 4$
- **B.** $x = -\frac{1}{4}$
- **C.** $x = -\frac{1}{4}, \frac{1}{4}$
- **D.** $x = 1, 4$
- **E.** $x = 4$

32. The area of a right triangle is 24.5 square centimeters. If one of its angles measures 45°, what is the length of its hypotenuse?

- **F.** 4.95 centimeters
- **G.** 7 centimeters
- **H.** 8.9 centimeters
- **J.** 9.9 centimeters
- **K.** 10 centimeters

33. Adam owns 4 times as many shirts as he has pairs of pants, and he has 5 pairs of pants for every 2 pairs of shoes. What is the ratio of Adam's shirts to Adam's shoes?

- **A.** 10 shirts : 1 pair shoes
- **B.** 15 shirts : 2 pairs shoes
- **C.** 20 shirts : 1 pair shoes
- **D.** 25 shirts : 1 pair shoes
- **E.** 25 shirts : 2 pairs shoes

34. Patrick is coming home from vacation in Costa Rica and wants to fill one of his suitcases with bags of Costa Rican coffee. The weight limit for his suitcase is 22 kilograms, and the suitcase itself weighs 3.2 kilograms. If each bag of coffee weighs 800 grams, how many bags can he bring in his suitcase without going over the limit?

- **F.** 2.00
- **G.** 2.75
- **H.** 4.00
- **J.** 23.00
- **K.** 27.00

35. Which of the following expressions can be simplified to $8x$?

- **A.** $10 - 2\left(\frac{x^2 - x}{x}\right) + 1$
- **B.** $\left(\frac{6 + 9}{7 - 4}\right)x + 9 - 6x$
- **C.** $\frac{(2x + 3)}{9^{\frac{1}{2}}} + x^3$
- **D.** $16\left(\frac{x^2}{2^{-1}}\right)$
- **E.** $\frac{48}{6 \times 4} + 2^3 x - \frac{4^{(9-6)}}{32}$

36. The number of college applicants increased in 2014 by 7%. This is 15% larger than the increase in 2013. What was the percentage increase in college applicants in 2013?

- **F.** 2%
- **G.** 4%
- **H.** 6%
- **J.** 8%
- **K.** 10%

37. Jess and Joe both took a math exam. Jess answered $\frac{7}{8}$ of the questions correctly. Joe answered 88% correctly. Who scored higher on the exam and by how much?

- **A.** Jess by 0.5%
- **B.** Joe by 0.5%
- **C.** Jess by $\frac{1}{16}$
- **D.** Joe by $\frac{1}{16}$
- **E.** There is not enough information.

38. Simplify: $\left(x^{\frac{1}{2}}\right)^{-3}$

   F. $x^{-1/2}$

   G. $x^{\frac{-5}{2}}$

   H. $\dfrac{1}{\sqrt{x^3}}$

   J. $\sqrt{x^3}$

   K. $-\sqrt{x^3}$

39. A 650 square foot apartment in Boston costs $1800 per month to rent. What is the monthly rent per square foot?

   A. $0.36

   B. $2.77

   C. $3.00

   D. $3.66

   E. $13.00

40. The average height of female students in a class is 64.5 inches, and the average height of male students in the class is 69 inches. If there are 1.5 times as many female students as male students, what is the average height for the entire class?

   F. 66.30 inches

   G. 66.75 inches

   H. 37.00 inches

   J. 67.20 inches

   K. 67.50 inches

41. A swimmer is swimming 25 meter sprints. If he swims 4 sprints in 3 minutes, 6 more sprints in 5 minutes, and then 4 final sprints in 2 minutes, what was his average speed during his sprints?

   A. 1.4 meters per minute

   B. 17.9 meters per minute

   C. 35 meters per minute

   D. 179 meters per minute

   E. 350 meters per minute

42. Julian is throwing a surprise birthday party for his best friend. He needs to purchase 240 cans of soda and 6 veggie platters. Soda cans are purchased in sets of 6 at price of $2.35 per pack. Veggie platters are sold in sets of 2 for $12.95. How much will he spend on sodas and vegetable platters?

   F. $132.85

   G. $135.75

   H. $162.90

   J. $184.87

   K. $641.70

43. Andy needs to make a pie and some cupcakes. He uses half of his butter to make the pie, and then uses a quarter of the remaining butter to make the cupcakes. If he has 2 cups of butter left, how much did he have before he made the pie?

   A. 4 cups

   B. 5.33 cups

   C. 6.5 cups

   D. 8 cups

   E. 8.5 cups

44. Which of the following mathematical expressions is equivalent to $\dfrac{2(x+y)}{z}$?

   F. $\frac{1}{z}(2x + 2y)$

   G. $\frac{x+y}{z} \times \frac{1}{2}$

   H. $\frac{2}{z} + \frac{x+y}{z}$

   J. $z(2x + 2y)$

   K. $\dfrac{2}{z(x+y)}$

45. If a rectangular field has a perimeter of 44 yards and a length of 36 feet, what is the field's width?

   A. 18 feet

   B. 30 feet

   C. 42 feet

   D. 4 yards

   E. 28 yards

46. A landscaping company charges 5 cents per square foot for fertilizer. How much would they charge to fertilize a 30 foot by 50 foot lawn?

   F. $7.50

   G. $15.00

   H. $75.00

   J. $150.00

   K. $750.00

47. The annual profits of Company A for 2000 – 2005 are shown in the graph below. How much did Company A's profit increase from 2003 to 2004?

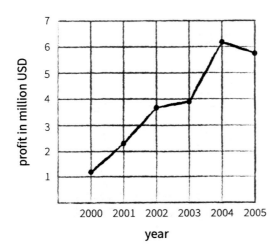

   A. $2.3 million

   B. $3.2 million

   C. $3.9 million

   D. $5.0 million

   E. $6.2 million

48. Which of the following is the equation of a circle with center at (0, 0) that passes through the point (5, 12) on the standard x, y-coordinate plane?

   F. $x + y = 169$

   G. $x - y = 13$

   H. $x^2 + y^2 = 13$

   J. $x^2 + y^2 = 169$

   K. $x^2 - y^2 = 169$

49. Which of the following expressions is equivalent to $(\frac{12}{3} \times 5.99) + (\frac{100}{20} \times 2.99)$?

   A. $\frac{5.99 \times 3}{12} + \frac{2.99 \times 20}{100}$

   B. $\frac{12 + 100}{5.99 + 2.99} \div (3 + 20)$

   C. $(5.99 + 2.99) \times \left(\frac{12}{3} + \frac{100}{20}\right)$

   D. $(5.99 + 2.99) \div \left(\frac{12}{3} + \frac{100}{20}\right)$

   E. $5.99 \times 12 \div 3 + 2.99 \times 100 \div 20$

50. The scores received by students on a recent science test are shown in the pie chart below. For this class, a score of 70 or above is required to pass the exam. According to the graph, what percentage of students passed this exam?

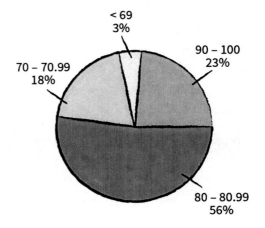

   F. 3 percent

   G. 18 percent

   H. 56 percent

   J. 69 percent

   K. 97 percent

51. Jesse rides her bike 2 miles south and 8 miles east. She then takes the shortest possible route back home. What was the total distance she traveled?

   A. 7.75 miles

   B. 8.25 miles

   C. 12.00 miles

   D. 17.75 miles

   E. 18.25 miles

52. Students in a particular math class received an average score of 84% on a recent test. If there are 20 boys and 30 girls in the class, and the boys' average score was 82%, what was the girls' average score?

F. 83%

G. 88%

H. 85%

J. 86%

K. 87%

53. What is an *x*-intercept of the graph $y = x^2 - 7x + 12$?

A. −4

B. 0

C. 3

D. 7

E. 12

54. Meg rolled a 6-sided die 4 times, and her first 3 rolls were 1, 3, and 5. If the average of the 4 rolls is 2.5, what was the result of the 4th roll?

F. 1

G. 2

H. 3

J. 5

K. 6

55. A circular swimming pool has a circumference of 49 feet. What is the diameter of the pool?

A. 7.8 feet

B. 8.2 feet

C. 12.3 feet

D. 15.6 feet

E. 17.8 feet

56. Three boats are positioned in a lake at points A, B, and C as shown below. Which of the following expressions gives the approximate distance, in meters, between Point A and Point C? (Note: For $\triangle DEF$, where *d*, *e*, and *f* are the lengths of the sides opposite $\angle D$, $\angle E$, and $\angle F$, respectively, $\frac{\sin\theta D}{d} = \frac{\sin\theta E}{e} = \frac{\sin\theta F}{f}$).

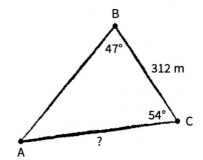

A. $\frac{312\sin47}{\sin79}$

B. $\frac{312\sin54}{\sin79}$

C. $\frac{312\sin79}{\sin47}$

D. $\frac{312\sin47}{\sin54}$

E. $\frac{312\sin54}{\sin47}$

57. A triangle has angles measuring 45°, 45°, and 90°. If one side length is 4 feet, what is the length of the hypotenuse?

A. 2.8 feet

B. 4.9 feet

C. 5.2 feet

D. 5.7 feet

E. 6.1 feet

58. One-way city bus tickets cost $1.75. The transportation department offers a monthly bus pass for $48. During the week, Jun commutes to work roundtrip on the bus. If Jun bought the monthly pass, how many days would he have to commute per month in order to save money?

    F. 7
    G. 10
    H. 14
    J. 20
    K. 28

59. If there are 380 female students in a graduating class, and male students represent 60% of the graduating class, how many total students are there in the class?

    A. 423
    B. 570
    C. 633
    D. 720
    E. 950

60. The slope of a straight line is −3 and its y-intercept is −2. Find the line's x-intercept.

    F. $x = -3$
    G. $x = -2$
    H. $x = -\frac{2}{3}$
    J. $x = 1\frac{1}{2}$
    K. $x = 2$

Answer Key: Mathematics

1.	E.	21.	C.	41.	C.
2.	G.	22.	F.	42.	F.
3.	D.	23.	C.	43.	D.
4.	G.	24.	G.	44.	F.
5.	B.	25.	B.	45.	B.
6.	H.	26.	H.	46.	H.
7.	C.	27.	A.	47.	A.
8.	F.	28.	K.	48.	J.
9.	C.	29.	A.	49.	E.
10.	K.	30.	J.	50.	K.
11.	D.	31.	B.	51.	E.
12.	F.	32.	J.	52.	H.
13.	B.	33.	E.	53.	C.
14.	K.	34.	J.	54.	F.
15.	B.	35.	B.	55.	D.
16.	H.	36.	H.	56.	F.
17.	C.	37.	A.	57.	D.
18.	F.	38.	H.	58.	H.
19.	B.	39.	B.	59.	E.
20.	K.	40.	F.	60.	H.

READING PRACTICE TEST

Literary Narrative: Excerpt from
Northanger Abbey by Jane Austen (1817)

Every morning now brought its regular duties—shops were to be visited; some new part of the town to be looked at; and the pump-room[1] to be attended, where they paraded up and down for an hour, looking at everybody and speaking to no one. The wish of a numerous acquaintance in Bath was still uppermost with Mrs. Allen, and she repeated it after every fresh proof, which every morning brought, of her knowing nobody at all.

They made their appearance in the Lower Rooms; and here fortune was more favourable to our heroine. The master of the ceremonies introduced to her a very gentlemanlike young man as a partner; his name was Tilney. He seemed to be about four or five and twenty, was rather tall, had a pleasing countenance, a very intelligent and lively eye, and, if not quite handsome, was very near it. His address was good, and Catherine felt herself in high luck. There was little leisure for speaking while they danced; but when they were seated at tea, she found him as agreeable as she had already given him credit for being. He talked with fluency and spirit—and there was an archness and pleasantry in his manner which interested, though it was hardly understood by her. After chatting some time on such matters as naturally arose from the objects around them, he suddenly addressed her with—"I have hitherto been very remiss, madam, in the proper attentions of a partner here; I have not yet asked you how long you have been in Bath; whether you were ever here before; whether you have been at the Upper Rooms, the theatre, and the concert; and how you like the place altogether. I have been very negligent—but are you now at leisure to satisfy me in these particulars? If you are I will begin directly."

"You need not give yourself that trouble, sir."

---

[1] The Grand Pump-Room and the Lower Rooms in England were meeting places for the upper class. People visiting might walk or dance.

"No trouble, I assure you, madam." Then forming his features into a set smile, and affectedly softening his voice, he added, with a simpering air, "Have you been long in Bath, madam?"

"About a week, sir," replied Catherine, trying not to laugh.

"Really!" with affected astonishment.

"Why should you be surprised, sir?"

"Why, indeed!" said he, in his natural tone. "But some emotion must appear to be raised by your reply, and surprise is more easily assumed, and not less reasonable than any other. Now let us go on. Were you never here before, madam?"

"Never, sir."

"Indeed! Have you yet honoured the Upper Rooms?"

"Yes, sir, I was there last Monday."

"Have you been to the theatre?"

"Yes, sir, I was at the play on Tuesday."

"To the concert?"

"Yes, sir, on Wednesday."

"And are you altogether pleased with Bath?"

"Yes—I like it very well."

"Now I must give one smirk, and then we may be rational again." Catherine turned away her head, not knowing whether she might venture to laugh. "I see what you think of me," said he gravely—"I shall make but a poor figure in your journal tomorrow."

"My journal!"

"Yes, I know exactly what you will say: Friday, went to the Lower Rooms; wore my sprigged muslin robe with blue trimmings—plain black shoes—appeared to much advantage; but was strangely harassed by a queer, half-witted man, who would make me dance with him, and distressed me by his nonsense."

"Indeed I shall say no such thing."

"Shall I tell you what you ought to say?"

"If you please."

"I danced with a very agreeable young man, introduced by Mr. King; had a great deal of conversation with him—seems a most extraordinary genius—hope I may know more of him. That, madam, is what I wish you to say."

"But, perhaps, I keep no journal."

"Perhaps you are not sitting in this room, and I am not sitting by you. These are points in which a doubt is equally possible. Not keep a journal! How are your absent cousins to understand the tenour of your life in Bath without one? How are the civilities and compliments of every day to be related as they ought to be, unless noted down every evening in a journal? How are your various dresses to be remembered, and the particular state of your complexion, and curl of your hair to be described in all their diversities, without having constant recourse to a journal? My dear madam, I am not so ignorant of young ladies' ways as you wish to believe me; it is this delightful habit of journaling which largely contributes to form the easy style of writing for which ladies are so generally celebrated. Everybody allows that the talent of writing agreeable letters is peculiarly female. Nature may have done something, but I am sure it must be essentially assisted by the practice of keeping a journal."

1. The point of view from which the passage is told can best be described as

   A. a young girl looking back fondly on the memories of her childhood

   B. a mother recalling the childhood of her daughter

   C. an unidentified narrator telling the story of a young woman's experiences in English society

   D. an unidentified narrator telling the story of a young man's first meeting of the girl he will marry

2. It can reasonably be inferred from the passage that which of the following represents a goal of Catharine Morland?

   F. joining good society in order to meet eligible young men

   G. establishing financial independence for herself

   H. representing her family's good name in diverse circumstances

   J. getting exercise in order to improve her health

3. It can reasonably be inferred from the passage that Mr. Tilney would agree with which of the following statements about other people he has met in the Lower Rooms?

   A. They are sincerely interested in the lives and conversation of their companions and the people they meet.

   B. Their conversation is shallow and repetitive, and this makes them uninteresting.

   C. They feel strongly about proper public and societal behavior and frequently enforce those standards.

   D. They are kind and care about their neighbors and friends and often enquire about their lives.

4. Which of the following best represents a summary of the encounter between Mr. Tilney and Catharine?

   F. A young woman meets a young man and they speak briefly of her day; she records the encounter in her journal that evening.

   G. A young man reads about the encounter his girlfriend has with a stranger at the Lower Rooms.

   H. A young woman meets a young man who flirts with her by mocking other acquaintances who have the same general conversations over and over.

   J. A young man meets a young woman who does not understand the appropriate conversation to have with a new acquaintance in the Lower Rooms.

5. It can reasonably be inferred from the passage that Mr. Tilney and Catharine might agree on which of the following statements?

   A. It is important to make new acquaintances in the Lower Rooms in order to advance one's social standing.

   B. It is important to dance well to attract an attractive and eligible partner.

   C. It Is important to keep a detailed journal in order to improve one's writing skills and memory.

   D. It is important to behave and speak appropriately to an interesting partner, to keep his or her interest.

6. Which of the following inferences about Catharine is supported by the passage?

   F. She is interested in meeting an eligible partner from the right society.

   G. She is shallow and only interested in appearances.

   H. She is inexperienced in talking to new acquaintances and does not know what to say.

   J. She will probably not speak to Mr. Tilney again in the future, because he was rude.

7. It can reasonably be inferred from Mr. Tilney's manner at the end of the first paragraph that he could be characterized as:

   A. rude and inconsiderate of the people around him.

   B. fanciful and imaginative about his partner's life.

   C. stuffy and unimaginative in his conversation.

   D. witty and self-confident about his own manner.

8. Which of the following statements about Mr. Tilney's attitude toward other young ladies of his acquaintance is supported by the passage?

   F. He finds them dull and uninteresting and wishes they would consider things besides the men they meet and the clothes they wear.

   G. He finds them charming and generally agreeable, although they focus too much on surface details in their observations.

   H. He finds their letters uninspiring and uninteresting because they always speak of other young men and clothing.

   J. He finds their company to be uninteresting, though he enjoys getting letters from his female cousins about their trips to Bath.

9. From the context, it can be inferred that the "master of ceremonies" is responsible for which actions?

   A. choosing who will attend the Lower and Upper Rooms

   B. providing entertainment for those who attend the Rooms

   C. planning refreshment for the guests of the Rooms

   D. providing suitable dance partners for those in the Rooms who do not have them

10. Based on the passage, which of the following most closely matches Catharine's goals for a successful trip to the Lower Rooms?

    F. a handsome dance partner and agreeable conversation

    G. new and interesting ideas gained from conversation

    H. a humorous discussion of one's neighbors

    J. a serious discussion about the shortcomings of one's society

Social Studies: Excerpt from the chapter "The Ch'in Dynasty (256-207 B.C.)" in *A History of China* (2004)
by Wolfram Eberhard

The territories of the state of Ch'in, the present Shensi and eastern Kansu, were from a geographical point of view transit regions, closed off in the north by steppes and deserts and in the south by almost impassable mountains. Only between these barriers, along the rivers Wei (in Shensi) and T'ao (in Kansu), is there a rich cultivable zone which is also the only means of transit from east to west. All traffic from and to Turkestan had to take this route. It is believed that strong relations with eastern Turkestan began in this period, and the state of Ch'in must have drawn big profits from its "foreign trade". The merchant class quickly gained more and more importance. The population was growing through immigration from the east which the government encouraged. This growing population with its increasing means of production, especially the great new irrigation systems, provided a welcome field for trade which was also furthered by the roads, though these were actually built for military purposes.

The state of Ch'in had never been so closely associated with the feudal communities of the rest of China as the other feudal states. A great part of its population, including the ruling class, was not purely Chinese but contained an admixture of Turks and Tibetans. The other Chinese even called Ch'in a "barbarian state", and the foreign influence was, indeed, unceasing. This was a favourable soil for the overcoming of feudalism, and the process was furthered by the factors mentioned in the preceding chapter, which were leading to a change in the social structure of China. Especially the recruitment of the whole population, including the peasantry, for war was entirely in the interest of the influential nomad fighting peoples within the state. About 250 B.C., Ch'in was not only one of the economically strongest among the feudal states, but had already made an end of its own feudal system.

Every feudal system harbours some seeds of a bureaucratic system of administration: feudal lords have their personal servants who are not recruited from the nobility, but who by their easy access to the lord can easily gain importance. They may, for instance, be put in charge of estates, workshops, and other properties of the lord and thus acquire experience in administration and an efficiency which are obviously of advantage to the lord. When Chinese lords of the preceding period, with the help of their sub-lords of the nobility, made wars, they tended to put the newly-conquered areas not into the hands of newly-enfeoffed noblemen, but to keep them as their property and to put their administration into the hands of efficient servants; these were the first bureaucratic officials. Thus, in the course of the later Chou period, a bureaucratic system of administration had begun to develop, and terms like "district" or "prefecture" began to appear, indicating that areas under a bureaucratic administration existed beside and inside areas under feudal rule. This process had gone furthest in Ch'in and was sponsored by the representatives of the Legalist School, which was best adapted to the new economic and social situation.

A son of one of the concubines of the penultimate feudal ruler of Ch'in was living as a hostage in the neighbouring state of Chao, in what is now northern Shansi. There he made the acquaintance of an unusual man, the merchant Lü Pu-wei, a man of education and of great political influence. Lü Pu-wei persuaded the feudal ruler of Ch'in to declare this son his successor. He also sold a girl to the prince to be his wife, and the son of this marriage was to be the famous and notorious Shih Huang-ti. Lü Pu-wei came with his protege to Ch'in, where he became his Prime Minister, and after the prince's death in 247 B.C. Lü Pu-wei became the regent for his young son Shih Huang-ti (then called Cheng). For the first time in Chinese history a merchant, a commoner, had reached one of the highest positions in the state. It is not known what sort of trade Lü Pu-wei had carried on, but probably he dealt in horses, the principal export of the state of Chao. As horses were an absolute necessity for the armies of that time, it is easy to imagine that a horse-dealer might gain great political influence.

Soon after Shih Huang-ti's accession Lü Pu-wei was dismissed, and a new group of advisers, strong supporters of the Legalist school, came into power. These new men began an active policy of conquest instead of the peaceful course which Lü Pu-wei had pursued. One campaign followed another in the years from 230 to 222, until all the feudal states had been conquered, annexed, and brought under Shih Huang-ti's rule.

11. According to the passage, who of the following represents a change in the way power was distributed in China?

 A. Lü Pu-wei

 B. Shih Huang-ti

 C. newly created noblemen

 D. the feudal leader of Ch'in

GO ON

12. Based on the passage, a primary cause of the disappearance of feudal structure in Ch'in was:

    F. the influence of other feudal states in China disappearing.

    G. the new irrigation system that led to greater wealth for the working class.

    H. the foreign influence from Turkestan and Tibet.

    J. the completion of a new road system for the military.

13. From the information provided in the first and second paragraphs, it can reasonably be inferred that

    A. other Chinese states did not like Ch'in because it was constantly changing.

    B. outside territories like Turkestan found the Chinese economic system to be backwards and outdated.

    C. Ch'in had no valuable exports except for military strength.

    D. Ch'in was unusual and forward-thinking compared to other Chinese states.

14. According to paragraph three, which of the following best describes the difference between a bureaucratic official and a nobleman?

    F. An official cares for a district at the charge of a higher lord, while a nobleman owns and administers a piece of land for himself.

    G. An official may be created by a lord, but a lord may not create another nobleman.

    H. An official can only be named from the merchant class, while a nobleman can be created from any class.

    J. An official is better at running a district efficiently, while a nobleman tends to spend excessively.

15. The passage indicates that Ch'in became an important leader for other Chinese districts because:

    A. the new Prime minister for all of China came from Ch'in.

    B. Ch'in was especially successful at replacing its feudal society and obtaining economic success.

    C. Ch'in was a strategic military stronghold, key to winning several wars.

    D. Ch'in joined with neighboring region Chao to annex several feudal states and absorb them.

16. The passage states that the bureaucratic system of rule gained popularity in part because:

    F. the feudal serfs rebelled against the feudal leaders and demanded a change.

    G. trading partners for China wanted a more just system of rule and put economic pressure on China.

    H. the lords who conquered new territories preferred to keep the land under the rule of a trusted servant rather than create holdings for new noblemen.

    J. the merchant class became so powerful that they were able to demand a system with more sharing of power.

17. Which of the following is a main idea expressed in the first paragraph?

    A. The lack of cultivable land in Ch'in kept it from growing very quickly.

    B. Several factors contributed to the rapid growth of the trade economy in Ch'in.

    C. The growing merchant class created a problem for the workers by taking their earnings.

    D. The lack of roads was an issue in attracting foreign trade.

18. It can be inferred from the passage that Lü Pu-wei brought his protégé to Ch'in because:

    F. he felt that the horse trade in Ch'in would be better than that in Chou.

    G. he thought the child needed to meet his father.

    H. he thought the son would make a better ruler than the father.

    J. he hoped to gain a position of power in the government through the child.

19. Based on the passage, a historian trying to understand the rapid change in Ch'in's economic and power structures would probably also want to research which of the following topics?

    A. Chinese international relations

    B. a history of Turkestan

    C. trade goods and routes in and out of Ch'in

    D. the structure of the Chinese military

20. Which of the following best expresses a main idea of the passage?

    F. The state of Ch'in was a key leader in the change from feudal to bureaucratic power systems and economic growth in China leading up to the Chou period.

    G. Chinese feudal leaders only reluctantly allowed the power structures in China to change, maintaining control of as much land as possible.

    H. Foreign influences on China led to drastic and unwelcome changes in power and economic structures leading up to the Chou period.

    J. Building roads and military infrastructure can lead to economic growth and improved systems of governance.

Humanities: This passage is adapted from the essay "Shakespeare on Scenery" by Oscar Wilde, in which he addresses the opinions of William Shakespeare on the available scenery in Elizabethan theater. It was taken from the book *A Critic in Pall Mall: Being Extracts from Reviews and Miscellanies* (1919, Methuen & Co. Ltd.), a collection of essays by the same author.

Excerpt from "Shakespeare on Scenery"
by Oscar Wilde

I have often heard people wonder what Shakespeare would say, could he see Mr. Irving's production of his *Much Ado About Nothing*, or Mr. Wilson Barrett's setting of his *Hamlet*. Would he take pleasure in the glory of the scenery and the marvel of the colour? Would he be interested in the Cathedral of Messina, and the battlements of Elsinore? Or would he be indifferent, and say the play, and the play only, is the thing?

Speculations like these are always pleasurable, and in the present case happen to be profitable also. For it is not difficult to see what Shakespeare's attitude would be; not difficult, that is to say, if one reads Shakespeare himself, instead of reading merely what is written about him.

Speaking, for instance, directly, as the manager of a London theatre, through the lips of the chorus in *Henry V.*, he complains of the smallness of the stage on which he has to produce the pageant of a big historical play, and of the want of scenery which obliges him to cut out many of its most picturesque incidents, apologises for the scanty number of supers who had to play the soldiers, and for the shabbiness of the properties, and, finally, expresses his regret at being unable to bring on real horses.

In the *Midsummer Night's Dream*, again, he gives us a most amusing picture of the straits to which theatrical managers of his day were reduced by the want of proper scenery. In fact, it is impossible to read him without seeing that he is constantly protesting against the two special limitations of the Elizabethan stage—the lack of suitable scenery, and the fashion of men playing women's parts, just as he protests against other difficulties with which managers of theatres have still to contend, such as actors who do not understand their words; actors who miss their cues; actors who overact their parts; actors who mouth; actors who gag; actors who play to the gallery, and amateur actors.

And, indeed, a great dramatist, as he was, could not but have felt very much hampered at being obliged continually to interrupt the progress of a play in order to send on someone to explain to the audience that the scene was to be changed to a particular place on the entrance of a particular character, and after his exit to somewhere else; that the stage was to represent the deck of a ship in a storm, or the interior of a Greek temple, or the streets of a certain town, to all of which inartistic devices Shakespeare is reduced, and for which he always amply apologizes. Besides this clumsy method, Shakespeare had two other substitutes for scenery—the hanging out of a placard, and his descriptions. The first of these could hardly have satisfied his passion for picturesqueness and his feeling for beauty, and certainly did not satisfy the dramatic critic of his day. But as regards the description, to those of us who look on Shakespeare not merely as a playwright but as a poet, and who enjoy reading him at home just as much as we enjoy seeing him acted, it may be a matter of congratulation that he had not at his command such skilled machinists as are in use now at the Princess's and at the Lyceum. For had Cleopatra's barge, for instance, been a structure of canvas and Dutch metal, it would probably have been painted over or broken up after the withdrawal of the piece, and, even had it survived to our own day, would, I am afraid, have become extremely shabby by this time. Whereas now the beaten gold of its poop is still bright, and the purple of its sails still beautiful; its silver oars are not tired of keeping time to the music of the flutes they follow, nor the Nereid's flower-soft hands of touching its silken tackle; the mermaid still lies at its helm, and still on its deck stand the boys with their coloured fans. Yet lovely as all Shakespeare's descriptive passages are, a description is in its essence undramatic. Theatrical audiences are far more impressed by what they look at than by what they listen to; and the modern dramatist, in having the surroundings of his play visibly presented to the audience when the curtain rises, enjoys an advantage for which Shakespeare often expresses his desire. It is true that Shakespeare's descriptions are not what descriptions are in modern plays—accounts of what the audience can observe for themselves; they are the imaginative method by which he creates in the mind of the spectators the image of that which he desires them to see. Still, the quality of the drama is action. It is always dangerous to pause for picturesqueness. And the introduction of self-explanatory scenery enables the modern method to be far more direct, while the loveliness of form and colour which it gives us, seems to me often to create an artistic temperament in the audience, and to produce that joy in beauty for beauty's sake, without which the great masterpieces of art can never be understood, to which, and to which only, are they ever revealed.

21. Which of the following is a reasonable inference about Elizabethan theater based on paragraph four?

   A. There were no professional actors.

   B. The setting and costumes were not helpful in creating a believable environment.

   C. Female actors were not skillful enough to play major parts.

   D. Playwrights couldn't afford fancy sets because they had to finance the plays themselves.

22. According to the author's argument, which of the following is true about Shakespeare's plays?

   F. They required elaborate sets to create the appropriate mood for the audience.

   G. They frequently criticized the scenery used by other playwrights.

   H. They lacked enough parts for female actors.

   J. They frequently included complaints about inadequate scenery, actors, or other issues.

23. Which of the following best summarizes the main problems the author sees for Shakespeare's scenery?

    A. Actors were not always adept at delivering Shakespeare's descriptive lines and stages were too small to support large sets.

    B. Available materials and artistry did not allow elaborate sets and too much description in a play could slow down the action.

    C. Theater-goers did not appreciate elaborate sets and actors were not willing to help construct them.

    D. Descriptions of scenery were not sufficient for audiences to understand the plays and theater patrons refused to pay for elaborate sets.

24. The main idea of the first two paragraphs is best summarized by which of the following statements?

    F. Directors of Shakespearean plays often wonder what Shakespeare might think about a specific version of one of his plays.

    G. Shakespearean plays put on today often look extremely different from those put on in Shakespeare's own time.

    H. Shakespeare's own plays deliver plenty of clues as to how important scenery was to him as a playwright.

    J. Most critics of Shakespeare's plays have not actually read the plays, only what others say about them.

25. Which of the following best describes the two issues addressed by the author?

    A. The Elizabethan theater faced many difficulties in creating scenery, and Shakespeare could address these either with placards or through spoken imagery.

    B. Actors in the Elizabethan period faced many issues, and Shakespeare addressed these by complaining about their acting in interviews.

    C. Elizabethan playwrights faced many rules about what they could write, and Shakespeare addressed this by inserting metaphorical complaints about the rules.

    D. Women in the Elizabethan period were not allowed to act, and Shakespeare addressed this by assigning women's roles to men.

26. Which of the following best describes a reason that the author feels that *it may be a matter of congratulation that he had not at his command such skilled machinists*?

    F. Without skilled machinists to build his sets, Shakespeare was forced to do it himself and produced even better sets as a result.

    G. Shakespeare's plays are so metaphorical and thoughtful that too-elaborate sets would take away from the main point of the play.

    H. The lack of elaborate sets led to elaborate imagery which can be more fully enjoyed by those who like to read the plays, not just see them performed.

    J. Without detailed sets and costuming, the actors were forced to become better at their delivery of the play's lines.

GO ON

27. Which of the following best describes a reasonable conclusion that can be drawn from the concession that *Shakespeare's descriptions are not what descriptions are in modern plays* but rather images he desires the audience to see?

   A. The descriptions have a less *undramatic* effect on the play than modern descriptions would.

   B. The descriptions are less effective than modern ones because the audience cannot use the scenery to help interpret them.

   C. The descriptions do not allow modern directors to effectively create sets now that the technology is available.

   D. The descriptions make the plays less interesting because they hinder the action of the play.

28. Which of the following best paraphrases the author's use of the example of Cleopatra's ship?

   F. Now, the set piece that represents Cleopatra's beautiful ship will never be destroyed or damaged.

   G. Now, the description of Cleopatra's beautiful ship can never be altered and will live on in memory.

   H. Now, no other playwrights will dare to describe Cleopatra's ship any differently, because the description is immortal.

   J. Now, the description of Cleopatra's ship will always be beautiful, while a physical ship would long ago have deteriorated.

29. Based on the passage, it is clear that the author feels modern scenery on the whole adds value to Shakespeare's plays because

   A. the sets add clarity of understanding to the plays, allowing audiences to follow the action more easily.

   B. the beauty created by modern scenery allows a greater appreciation for art and beauty in the audience.

   C. the beauty of the sets compliments the simplicity of the play's lines.

   D. the sets are more easily manipulated and help improve the action of the play.

30. Overall, the author's attitude toward Shakespeare's plays is

   F. admiring, because he worked around many weaknesses to still produce beauty.

   G. critical, because Shakespeare often complains of difficulties in his plays.

   H. indifferent, because while Shakespeare is well-known, his plays are difficult to understand.

   J. apologetic, because his plays could have been much better if he had better scenery.

Excerpt from *More Science from an Easy Chair*
by Sir E. Ray (Edwin Ray) Lankester

What is laughter? It is a spasmodic movement of various muscles of the body, beginning with those which half close the eyes and those which draw backwards and upwards the sides of the mouth, and open it so as to expose the teeth, next affecting those of respiration so as to produce short rapidly succeeding expirations accompanied by sound (called "guffaws" when in excess) and then extending to the limbs, causing up and down movement of the half-closed fists and stamping of the feet, and ending in a rolling on the ground and various contortions of the body. Clapping the hands is not part of the laughter "process," but a separate, often involuntary, action which has the calling of attention to oneself as its explanation, just as slapping the ground or a table or one's thigh has. Laughter is spontaneous, that is to say, the movements are not designed or directed by the conscious will. But in mankind, in proportion as individuals are trained in self-control, it is more or less completely under command, and in spite of the most urgent tendency of the automatic mechanism to enter upon the progressive series of movements which we distinguish as (1) smile, (2) broad smile or grin, (3) laugh, (4) loud laughter, (5) paroxysms of uncontrolled laughter, a man or woman can prevent all indication by muscular movement of a desire to laugh or even to smile. Usually laughter is excited by certain pleasurable emotions, and is to be regarded as an "expression" of such emotion just as certain movements and the flow of tears are an "expression" of the painful emotion of grief and physical suffering, and as other movements of the face and limbs are an "expression" of anger, others of "fear." The Greek gods of Olympus enjoyed "inextinguishable laughter."

It is interesting to see how far we can account for the strange movements of laughter as part of the inherited automatic mechanism of man. Why do we laugh? What is the advantage to the individual or the species of "laughing"? Why do we "express" our pleasurable emotion and why in this way? It is said that the outcast diminutive race of Ceylon known as the Veddas never laugh, and it has even been seriously but erroneously stated that the muscles which move the face in laughter are wanting in them. A planter induced some of these people to camp in his "compound," or park, in order to learn something of their habits, language, and beliefs. One day he said to the chief man of the little tribe, "You Veddas never laugh. Why do you never laugh?" The little wild man replied, "It is true; we never laugh. What is there for us to laugh at?"—an answer almost terrible in its pathetic submission to a joyless life. For laughter is primarily, to all races and conditions of men, the accompaniment, the expression of the simple joy of life. It has acquired a variety of relations and significations in the course of the long development of conscious man—but primarily it is an expression of emotion, set going by the experience of the elementary joys of life—the light and heat of the sun, the approach of food, of love of triumph.

Before we look further into the matter it is well to note some exceptional cases of the causation of laughter. The first of these is the excitation of laughter by a purely mechanical "stimulus" or action from the exterior, without any corresponding mental emotion of joy—namely by "tickling," that is to say, by light rubbing or touching of the skin under the arms or at the side of the neck, or on the soles of the feet. Yet a certain readiness to respond is necessary on the part of the person who is "tickled," for, although an unwilling subject may be thus made to laugh, yet there are conditions of mind and of body in which "tickling" produces no response. I do not propose to discuss why it is that "tickling," or gentle friction of the skin produces laughter. It is probably one of those cases in which a mechanism of the living body is set to work, as a machine may be, by directly causing the final movement (say the turning of a wheel), for the production of which a special train of apparatus, to be started by the letting loose of a spring or the turning of a steam-cock, is provided, and in ordinary circumstance is the regular mode in which the working of the mechanism is started. The apparatus of laughter is when due to "tickling" set at work by a short cut to the nerves and related muscles without recourse to the normal emotional steam-cock.

GO ON

31. Which of the following best describes the main purpose of this passage?

    A. to describe the difference between voluntary and involuntary laughter

    B. to give an imaginative description of what laughter looks like

    C. to give a physical description of the process of laughing

    D. to offer a philosophical reasoning for why we laugh

32. The main idea of the second paragraph can best be expressed by which of the following statements?

    F. Varied explanations exist for why people laugh, but there is a clear connection to basic emotion.

    G. Because there are some groups of people who never laugh, it is clear that laughter is not a necessary or survival trait for people.

    H. People who do not laugh do not experience important, basic human emotions.

    J. It is impossible to determine why people laugh because most people do not laugh for the same reasons.

33. According to the passage, one physical symptom of laughter is:

    A. long, careful breaths that produce a gasping sound

    B. quick, shallow breaths that lead to sound

    C. creating a downward pull on the facial features

    D. clapping hands to create accompanying sound

34. Which of the following best describes the author's purpose for describing laughter in the first paragraph as a group of physical responses or symptoms?

    F. to demonstrate that most people do not understand laughter

    G. to illustrate the grotesqueness of the act of laughing

    H. to isolate the specific causes of laughter

    J. to demonstrate the complex and instinctual physical components of laughter

35. Which of the following statements about laughter would the author be LEAST likely to agree with?

    A. Laughter is a complex physical action that is little understood and almost entirely instinctual, though voluntary.

    B. Most people cannot explain why they laugh at a specific joke or occurrence.

    C. By examining the physical attributes of laughter, it is possible to understand the emotional stimulus that causes laughter.

    D. Laughter is a voluntary reaction to either physical or emotional stimulus.

36. The last paragraph suggests that tickling:

    F. is an expression of joy or happiness

    G. causes laughter through emotional stimulus

    H. causes laughter because it is similar to the first physical symptom of laughter

    J. simulates the final step in the process of laughter

37. The phrase the "apparatus of laughter" most nearly means which of the following?

    A. the measurement of intensity of laughter

    B. the process of laughter

    C. the machine of laughter

    D. the body parts affected by laughter

38. The example of the Veddas serves to reinforce the idea that:

F. laughter is an involuntary action

G. joyful emotion is a primary cause of laughter

H. there is little in life to laugh about

J. no two people laugh about the same things

39. Which of the following explains why being tickled should be considered an exception when discussing the primary causes of laughter?

A. It is similar to other causes of laughter already discussed and does not merit its own consideration.

B. It cannot be measured, so considering it as a stimulus is not possible.

C. It is provoked by the actions of other people rather than the individual, so it is impossible to correlate it to other causes.

D. It is provoked by a physical stimulus rather than a mental one, so it does not seem to follow the same process.

40. According to the passage, a person should be able to suppress signs of laughter by suppressing which of the following?

F. muscle movements

G. emotional responses

H. auditory responses

J. impulsive actions

Answer Key: Reading

1.	C.	15.	B.	29.	B.
2.	F.	16.	H.	30.	F.
3.	B.	17.	B.	31.	C.
4.	H.	18.	J.	32.	F.
5.	D.	19.	C.	33.	B.
6.	F.	20.	F.	34.	J.
7.	D.	21.	B.	35.	C.
8.	G.	22.	J.	36.	J.
9.	D.	23.	B.	37.	B.
10.	F.	24.	H.	38.	G.
11.	A.	25.	A.	39.	D.
12.	H.	26.	H.	40.	F.
13.	D.	27.	A.		
14.	F.	28.	J.		

SCIENCE PRACTICE TEST

Passage One

Biodiesel is a type of fuel that can be produced by mixing vegetable oil with methanol and a catalyst. Vegetable oil contains triglycerides, which are made of 3 fatty acids bound to 1 glycerol molecule. When triglycerides react with methanol, the fatty acids break off the glycerol molecule, and each one binds to one methanol molecule; this process is called a transesterification reaction. Normally, this reaction is very slow, so the catalyst potassium hydroxide (KOH) is used to increase the speed of the reaction.

This reaction makes two products. The fatty acids bound to methanol form the first product, biodiesel. The remaining glycerol and any free fatty acids react with excess KOH to form a byproduct, glycerin. Glycerin can be used to make soap.

Three experiments were conducted to compare various conditions for producing biodiesel. In experiment 1, the researcher heated 200mL of new vegetable oil to 55^{0}C. Meanwhile, she dissolved 1.3g of KOH catalyst in a beaker of methanol. Once dissolved, she carefully poured the methanol-KOH solution into the heated oil. She continued stirring for 45 minutes, then left the mixture to cool overnight. She conducted this procedure with four different quantities of methanol. When she came back the next morning, she found that all four mixtures had separated into two layers: a dark layer of glycerin on the bottom and a clear yellow layer of biodiesel on top. By dividing the volume of the top layer by the volume of oil used, she was able to calculate a percent yield of biodiesel for each.

Table 9.1. Experiment One

	TEMPERATURE	METHANOL	KOH CATALYST	OIL	% YIELD
TRIAL 1	55°C	20 mL	1.3 g	new	35
TRIAL 2	55°C	30 mL	1.3 g	new	50
TRIAL 3	55°C	40 mL	1.3 g	new	70
TRIAL 4	55°C	50 mL	1.3 g	new	70

In Experiment Two, the researcher increased the temperature of the oil to 68°C, and varied the amounts of methanol.

Table 9.2. Experiment Two

	TEMPERATURE	METHANOL	KOH CATALYST	OIL	% YIELD
TRIAL 1	68°C	40 mL	1.3 g	new	40
TRIAL 2	68°C	75 mL	1.3 g	new	60
TRIAL 3	68°C	90 mL	1.3 g	new	70

In Experiment Three, the researcher used old fryer oil instead of new vegetable oil. (Old oil usually contains more free fatty acids.) She heated the old oil to 55°C, used 40mL of methanol, and varied the amounts of KOH catalyst

Table 9.3. Experiment Three

	TEMPERATURE	METHANOL	KOH CATALYST	OIL	% YIELD
TRIAL 1	55°C	40 mL	1.3 g	old	30
TRIAL 2	55°C	40 mL	2.1 g	old	40
TRIAL 3	55°C	40 mL	2.8 g	old	70

1. In experiment 1, what amount of methanol produces the most biodiesel without wasting methanol?

   A. 20 mL

   B. 40 mL

   C. 30 mL

   D. 50 mL

2. In experiment 2, what is the effect of the higher temperature?

   F. At a higher temperature, more KOH catalyst is needed for a maximum percent yield.

   G. At a higher temperature, the percent yield is higher for a given amount of methanol.

   H. At a higher temperature, more methanol is needed for a maximum percent yield.

   J. At a higher temperature, more KOH catalyst is needed for a given amount of methanol.

3. Which of the following could explain the effect of higher temperature on the percent yield?

   A. At a higher temperature, more of the KOH catalyst dissolves in the methanol.

   B. At a higher temperature, some of the methanol boils off and is unavailable for the reaction.

   C. At a higher temperature, biodiesel is denser than glycerin.

   D. At a higher temperature, less glycerin is formed.

4. In experiment 3, what is the effect of using old oil?

   F. With old oil, more KOH catalyst is needed for a maximum percent yield.

   G. With old oil, higher temperatures are required for a maximum percent yield.

   H. With old oil, less KOH catalyst is needed for a given temperature.

   J. With old oil, less methanol is needed for a maximum percent yield.

5. Which of the following could explain the effect of using old oil on the percent yield?

    A. Old oil has a higher boiling point than new oil.

    B. Old oil contains more free fatty acids, which consume some of the KOH and leave less available to catalyze the reaction.

    C. Old oil is more reactive than new oil, and requires less KOH catalyst.

    D. Old oil contains more glycerol, which produces a greater proportion of glycerin.

6. How much more KOH catalyst is needed to produce a 70% yield of biodiesel using 40mL of old fryer oil compared to using 40mL of new vegetable oil?

    F. 2.8g

    G. 2.1g

    H. 1.5g

    J. 1.3g

7. Why does the glycerin separate into the bottom layer and the biodiesel into the top layer?

    A. Because there is more glycerin than biodiesel.

    B. Because glycerin is more watery than biodiesel.

    C. Because glycerin is produced first in the reaction.

    D. Because glycerin is denser than biodiesel.

8. The researcher repeated experiment 1 with 60mL of methanol and still got a 70% yield. Which of the following could explain why?

    F. Using more methanol produces more biodiesel and more glycerin in equal proportion.

    G. Using more methanol makes the transesterification reaction proceed more slowly.

    H. Excess methanol evaporates and decreases the volume of glycerin.

    J. Without increasing the amount of oil used, using more methanol cannot produce more biodiesel.

Passage Two

Blood type refers to the presence of certain antigens, also called blood group factors, on the surface of human blood cells. People who have factor A on their blood cells are said to have Type A blood. People who have factor B on their blood cells are said to have Type B blood. People who have both factors present are Type AB, and people with neither factor present have Type O blood.

Blood type is very important for determining which kind of blood is safe to donate from one person to another. People whose blood cells do not normally have factor A will react negatively to a transfusion of Type A blood because their immune system recognizes those cells as foreign. Likewise, people whose blood cells do not normally have factor B will react negatively to Type B blood. People with Type O blood react negatively to Type A, Type B, and Type AB; they can only receive Type O blood. People with Type AB blood can receive any blood type.

To test someone's blood type, a small amount of blood is drawn for agglutination tests (agglutination means clumping). First, a drop of blood is added to a test tube containing anti-A antibodies. If the blood cells have factor A present, they will form visible clumps with the anti-A antibodies. Next, a drop of blood is added to a different test tube containing anti-B antibodies. If the blood cells have factor B present, they will form visible clumps with the anti-B antibodies.

The tables below show agglutination test results for four different patients. A positive result means that clumps formed; a negative result means that no clumps formed.

Table 9.4. Agglutination Results

PATIENT	ANTI-A TEST	ANTI-B TEST
Caroline	Negative	Negative
Rich	Positive	Negative
Mary	Positive	Positive
Scott	Negative	Positive

9. Why did Rich's blood give a positive result for the anti-A agglutination test and a negative result for the anti-B agglutination test?

   A. Rich's blood cells have neither factor A nor factor B present.

   B. Rich's blood cells have factor A but not factor B present.

   C. Rich's blood cells have factor B but not factor A present.

   D. Rich's blood cells have both factor A and factor B present.

10. What is Caroline's blood type?

   F. Type A

   G. Type B

   H. Type AB

   J. Type O

11. What is Mary's blood type?

   A. Type A

   B. Type B

   C. Type AB

   D. Type O

12. From whom can Mary safely receive a blood donation?

   F. Caroline only

   G. Rich and Scott only

   H. Caroline, Rich, and Scott

   J. Mary cannot safely receive anyone else's blood.

13. From whom can Caroline safely receive a blood donation?

   A. Mary only

   B. Rich and Scott only

   C. Mary, Rich, and Scott

   D. Caroline cannot safely receive anyone else's blood.

14. Which of the following best explains the reason that Scott cannot receive a blood donation from Mary?

   F. Factor A on Mary's blood cells would be recognized as foreign by Scott's immune system.

   G. Factor B on Mary's blood cells would be recognized as foreign by Scott's immune system.

   H. Both factor A and factor B on Mary's blood cells would be recognized as foreign by Scott's immune system.

   J. Scott can only receive a donation of his identical blood type.

15. If a person had a previously undiscovered factor, called factor C, present on their blood cells, but no other factors present, whose blood type would this person's blood most resemble based on the agglutination tests shown above?

   A. Caroline

   B. Rich

   C. Mary

   D. Scott

16. Type O blood is called the "universal donor." Which of the following best explains why?

   F. People with Type O blood can receive all blood types.

   G. No blood type will have a negative reaction to receiving Type O blood.

   H. Type O blood is recognized as foreign by in people with type AB blood.

   J. Type O blood can only be donated to people who are Type O.

Passage Three

Sociobiology is the study of how evolution has shaped social behavior. While a scientist studying evolutionary biology may be interested in how humans evolved to walk on two feet, a sociobiologist would be more interested in how human evolution has shaped modern-day warfare and social roles. Evolution is shaped by natural selection, the principle which states that for genetic traits which vary in a population, individuals with traits better suited for survival will live longer and produce more offspring, which will lead to those traits being more common in the population over time. Sociobiology claims that just as natural selection led to birds evolving lightweight, hollow bones (better for flight), natural selection also led to humans evolving certain social behaviors. This theory argues that many human behaviors are therefore innate (the way a person is born), rather than cultural or environmental.

Edward O. Wilson, the father of sociobiology, argued that humans, like other animals, are under evolutionary pressures to protect their gene pool. This means that humans try to protect their family members, especially their children, because this will ensure that more of their genetic material will be passed along to future generations. Wilson went one step further, arguing that not only will humans try to protect their kin, but they will also naturally try to destroy those who are not like them, in order to reduce the competition for resources and to advance their own gene pool. This, Wilson claimed, explains why xenophobia is an innate human trait, and why countries continue to wage war against one another.

When Wilson first introduced his theory, he was met with vocal opposition. One of his major critics was Stephen Jay Gould, an evolutionary biologist who argued that Wilson's theory was based more on politics than on scientific fact. Gould claimed that human social behavior was shaped much more by societal and cultural factors (what you are taught) than by evolution. Evolution is a very slow process, Gould insisted, much too slow to account for the rapid changes in human societal structures that have occurred over the course of only a few generations. While Wilson claimed that the majority of leadership positions in human society will always be occupied by men because men are innately more dominant, Gould argued that Wilson's viewpoint was distorted by his personal prejudices. According to Gould, Wilson accepted male dominance not because it had been proven by science but because it was the social norm at the time. Gould believed that gender equality could be just as evolutionarily advantageous (if not more so) as male dominance. Moreover, Gould considered Wilson's theory to be dangerous in that it provided an unfounded, pseudoscientific justification for injustice, violence, and war.

GO ON

17. Which of the following best describes the difference between evolutionary biology and sociobiology?

    A. Evolutionary biology is a study of non-human animals; sociobiology is a study of humans.

    B. Evolutionary biology is a study of anatomy; sociobiology is a study of social behavior.

    C. Evolutionary biology is a very slow process; sociobiology affects changes much more quickly.

    D. Evolutionary biology explains how species diverge; sociobiology explains how species are similar.

18. Why, according to Wilson, do humans take so much care to protect their children?

    F. If they protect their children, their children will protect them.

    G. If they protect their children, the total population will increase in size.

    H. If they protect their children, there is more of a chance that their children will have children.

    J. If they protect their children, their children will be less independent.

19. Based on the passage, what does the word *xenophobia* mean?

    A. The fear of those with genetic material dissimilar to one's own

    B. The fear of violence

    C. The fear of being ostracized from one's social group

    D. The fear of going outside

20. Which of the following best explains why Gould criticized Wilson's theory?

    F. Gould thought Wilson's theory placed too much importance on cultural factors.

    G. Gould did not believe in evolution.

    H. Gould thought Wilson's theory applied to early human societies but not to modern societies.

    J. Gould thought Wilson's theory was unscientific and prejudiced.

21. Which of the following observations, if true, would lend evidence to Wilson's theory?

    A. In societies across the world, men have always been the "providers" and women have always cared for the children.

    B. As history has progressed, the number of countries waging war has decreased.

    C. Many animal species have social hierarchical structures.

    D. Modern societies have gone through radical changes due to political and social movements.

22. Wilson's central argument is that human social behavior is shaped by natural selection. To accept this theory, all of the following assumptions must be true except:

    F. There is a variety of human social behaviors throughout the species.

    G. An individual human's social behavior affects the likelihood that he or she will produce offspring.

    H. Children learn how to behave in society based on positive or negative reinforcement of their behavior by the community.

    J. Certain social behaviors are encoded in genes that are passed from parents to their offspring.

23. Although Wilson was mostly concerned with humans, sociobiology could also be applied to other species. Which of the following would be an example of sociobiology in non-human animals?

    A. A brown-coated deer rat population that migrated from a soil environment to a sandy environment evolved a sandy-colored coat to hide better from predators.

    B. Worker honeybees seem to know their role from birth, and they begin engaging in worker bee tasks in as little as 10 days after hatching.

    C. Some chimpanzees can be taught to communicate via sign language.

    D. Wild-born animals held in captivity can be trained to be more submissive.

24. Why did Gould believe that sociobiology as a theory could be dangerous?

    F. The idea that current social hierarchies are innate could be used as a reason to preserve inequalities within society.

    G. The idea that humans evolve like other species could mean that humans are not as special as we think.

    H. The idea that parents pass behaviors on to their children could be used as a reason to punish parents for their children's crimes.

    J. The idea that humans are under evolutionary pressures to protect their children could be used as a reason to justify nepotism.

Passage Four

A physics student conducts a series of experiments with a simple pendulum. He constructs the pendulum by hanging a small mass to the end of a length of string, and tying the top of the string to a horizontal rod supported by a stand. For each trial, he pulls the mass away from the vertical and releases. He times 30 seconds and counts how many times the mass makes a full oscillation (swinging back to its starting point). He divides this number by 30 seconds to find the frequency. In experiment 1, he varies the length of string, in experiment 2, he varies the mass, and in experiment 3 he varies the angle of release. His results are shown in the tables below.

Table 9.5. Experiment One: Varying String Length

	ANGLE OF RELEASE	MASS	STRING LENGTH	NUMBER OF OSCILLATIONS (in 30 seconds)	FREQUENCY (oscillations per second)
TRIAL 1	10°	10 g	10 cm	47	1.6
TRIAL 2	10°	10 g	15 cm	38	1.3
TRIAL 3	10°	10 g	20 cm	33	1.1

Table 9.6. Experiment Two: Varying Mass

	ANGLE OF RELEASE	MASS	STRING LENGTH	NUMBER OF OSCILLATIONS (in 30 seconds)	FREQUENCY (oscillations per second)
TRIAL 1	10°	10 g	15 cm	38	1.3
TRIAL 2	10°	20 g	15 cm	38	1.3
TRIAL 3	10°	30 g	15 cm	38	1.3

Table 9.7. Experiment Three: Varying Angles of Release

	ANGLE OF RELEASE	MASS	STRING LENGTH	NUMBER OF OSCILLATIONS (in 30 seconds)	FREQUENCY (oscillations per second)
TRIAL 1	5°	10 g	15 cm	38	1.3
TRIAL 2	10°	10 g	15 cm	38	1.3
TRIAL 3	15°	10 g	15 cm	37	1.2

25. What of the following is true about the effect of string length on the motion of a simple pendulum?

 A. As the string length increases, the pendulum takes less time to swing from side to side.

 B. As the string length increases, the pendulum takes more time to swing from side to side.

 C. As the string length increases, the pendulum swings higher to each side.

 D. As the string length increases, the pendulum gains more potential energy.

26. What of the following is true about the effect of mass on the motion of a simple pendulum?

 F. As the mass increases, the pendulum takes more time to swing from side to side.

 G. As the mass decreases, the pendulum swings higher to each side.

 H. As the mass increases, the pendulum completes more oscillations in a given amount of time.

 J. Mass has no effect on the motion of a simple pendulum.

27. If the student were to repeat his experiment with an angle of 5°, a mass of 10g and a string length of 25 cm, what would you estimate to be the frequency?

 A. 0.6 oscillations per second

 B. 1.0 oscillations per second

 C. 1.2 oscillations per second

 D. 1.4 oscillations per second

28. If the student were to repeat his experiment with an angle of 5°, a mass of 30g and a string length of 10 cm, what would you estimate to be the frequency?

 F. 0.9 oscillations per second

 G. 1.1 oscillations per second

 H. 1.3 oscillations per second

 J. 1.6 oscillations per second

29. What of the following is true about the effect of the angle of release on the motion of a simple pendulum?

 A. At angles below 20°, increasing the angle makes the pendulum swing faster.

 B. At angles below 20°, increasing the angle makes the pendulum swing slower.

 C. At angles below 20°, the angle has a negligible effect on the frequency.

 D. At angles below 20°, the angle has a negligible effect on the height of the oscillation.

30. The period (T) is the inverse of the frequency. Which of the following is true of T?

 F. T is directly proportional to string length.

 G. T is directly proportional to mass.

 H. T is inversely proportional to string length.

 J. T is inversely proportional to mass.

31. Imagine that the student repeated his experiments on the moon, where the force of gravity is much smaller, and found that the frequency was higher for all trials. Which of the following is true of T?

   A. T is directly proportional to the force of gravity.

   B. T is indirectly proportional to the force of gravity.

   C. T is directly proportional to the weight of the mass.

   D. The weight of the mass has no effect on T.

32. Why do you think the student counted the number of oscillations for 30 seconds rather than timing one single oscillation to find the frequency?

   F. It takes approximately 30 seconds for the pendulum to reach a constant angular velocity.

   G. Each oscillation takes a different amount of time, so it is better to find an average.

   H. Each oscillation reaches a different height, so it is better to find an average.

   J. Counting oscillations over a period of time and dividing by that time reduces the chance of error.

Passage Five

Edwin Hubble was an American astronomer who, in 1929, observed that galaxies were moving away from each other in every direction at speeds proportional to their distance from the earth. His discovery that the universe was expanding excited a lot of astronomers and cosmologists, and opened the doors to new theories about how the universe was created. Georges Lemaître, a Belgian priest and physicist, proposed his "hypothesis of the primeval atom" in 1931. If the universe was expanding, Lemaître argued, one must be able to trace it back to a single point of origin. Lemaître called this initial point the "primeval atom," and he claimed that an explosion of the primeval atom was what first created the universe. His theory became later known as the Big Bang theory.

Although the Big Bang theory is now widely accepted by scientists, this was not always the case. Fred Hoyle, an English astronomer, criticized Lemaître's theory. In fact, it was Hoyle who mockingly coined the phrase "the Big Bang." He thought the idea of one explosion creating the entire universe was ridiculous. Hoyle argued that there was no finite beginning, nor an end, to the universe. He and his colleagues Bondi and Gold developed the Steady-State theory, which stated that the universe must be uniform throughout time and space in order for the laws of physics to work the same way in all parts of the universe. Hoyle acknowledged that the universe was expanding, as Hubble had discovered, but he argued that the density of the universe did not change since matter was being continuously created at a rate that matched the expansion.

Two major discoveries in the decades that followed provided more evidence for the Big Bang theory and ushered out the Steady-State theory. The first was the observation of quasars. Quasars, first discovered in the 1960s, are incredibly bright regions in the center of galaxies surrounding supermassive black holes. Quasars are so far away that their light takes several billion years to reach the earth. The discovery of quasars was proof that a few billion years ago, when quasars were first created, the structure of the universe must have been much different than it is today. The second discovery was that of cosmic microwave background (CMB) radiation. Arno Penzias and Robert Wilson discovered CMB by accident while they were using a radiometer to study satellite communication. They kept recording a very high frequency microwave, which at first they thought might have been caused by pigeon droppings on their antennas. The two scientists later discovered that this microwave was much lower energy than any radiation emitted by our galaxy, and that it was likely radiation left over from the Big Bang explosion.

33. Which of the following best describes the basis on which Lemaître first developed his primeval atom hypothesis?

   A. The presence of high frequency microwave radiation is proof that the universe was created by a radioactive explosion.

   B. The fact that the universe looks the same in all places at all times is proof that its density does not change.

   C. The fact that the universe is constantly expanding implies that its expansion could be traced back to a point of origin.

   D. The fact that quasars exist is proof that the universe is at least several billion years old.

34. What was the major reason why Hoyle rejected Lemaître's theory?

   F. Hoyle believed the universe was uniform throughout time and space.

   G. Hoyle believed the universe was not expanding as quickly as Lemaître claimed.

   H. Hoyle believed the universe had a beginning but not a foreseeable end.

   J. Hoyle believed the universe was getting more dense.

35. Which of the following statements is consistent with both Lemaître's and Hoyle's theories about the universe?

   A. Matter is continuously created in the universe.

   B. The oldest elements in the universe are those that are the farthest away.

   C. Although the size of the universe is changing, the density of the universe remains the same.

   D. The galaxies of the universe are continuously receding.

36. Which of the following best explains the significance of the discovery of quasars?

   F. The observation that quasars are uniformly distributed throughout the universe supported the Steady-State theory.

   G. The observation that quasars surround supermassive black holes supported the Big Bang theory.

   H. The observation that quasars are located several billion light years away supported the Big Bang theory.

   J. The observation that quasars emit high frequency radiation supported the Big Bang theory.

37. Which of the following best explains the relationship between Hubble's discovery and the Big Bang and Steady-State theories?

   A. Hubble's discovery that the universe was expanding directly contradicted the Steady-State theory.

   B. Hubble's discovery that the universe was expanding directly contradicted the Big Bang theory.

   C. Hubble's discovery that the universe was expanding was consistent with both the Big Bang and Steady-State theories.

   D. Hubble's discovery that the universe was expanding was not generally accepted as scientific fact until the Big Bang theory provided proof.

38. Which of the following best explains the significance of the discovery of cosmic microwave background (CMB) radiation?

   F. The observation that CMB was found uniformly throughout the universe supported the Steady-State theory.

   G. The observation that CMB was too low energy to be from our galaxy supported the Big Bang theory.

   H. The observation that CMB was several billion light years away supported the Big Bang theory.

   J. The observation that CMB was emitted by our galaxy, but not by other galaxies, supported the Big Bang theory.

39. Hoyle's Steady-State theory claimed that the universe was both dynamic and uniform. How, according to Hoyle, could it be both?

    A. Although the universe is continuously expanding, matter is continuously created to fill in the gaps.

    B. Although the universe is continuously expanding from the perspective of those on Earth, it is actually shrinking from the perspective of other galaxies.

    C. Although new matter is continuously created, old stars and galaxies are continuously consumed by black holes.

    D. Although the universe is continuously expanding, it is doing so at a constant velocity.

40. Which of the following characterizes one of the reasons that Steady-State theory is no longer a popular theory?

    F. Scientists have discovered that the expansion of the universe is accelerating.

    G. Scientists have discovered that the expansion of the universe has very little to do with its density.

    H. Scientists have discovered that the universe is much older than Hoyle believed.

    J. Scientists have discovered that the universe is not as uniform as Hoyle believed.

Answer Key: Science

1.	B.	**15.**	A.	**29.**	C.
2.	H.	**16.**	G.	**30.**	F.
3.	B.	**17.**	B.	**31.**	B.
4.	F.	**18.**	H.	**32.**	J.
5.	B.	**19.**	A.	**33.**	C.
6.	H.	**20.**	J.	**34.**	F.
7.	D.	**21.**	A.	**35.**	D.
8.	J.	**22.**	H.	**36.**	H.
9.	B.	**23.**	B.	**37.**	C.
10.	J.	**24.**	F.	**38.**	G.
11.	C.	**25.**	B.	**39.**	A.
12.	H.	**26.**	J.	**40.**	J.
13.	D.	**27.**	B.		
14.	F.	**28.**	J.		

ten

WRITING
PRACTICE TEST

Read the passage and consider the following perspectives. Each suggests a particular way of thinking about the growth of the oil extraction industry. Write an essay in which you evaluate multiple perspectives on the importance and consequence of oil extraction. In your essay, you should

◇ **evaluate the perspectives given below**

◇ **explain your own position on the issue**

◇ **detail how your perspective compares to the others given**

Economic Development and Growth in Storm-Prone Areas

In recent years, catastrophic hurricanes, typhoons, and cyclones around the world have resulted in large-scale destruction and loss of life. However, rapid population growth and the urban development necessary to accommodate it have continued in areas vulnerable to storms and flooding, putting millions at risk. In addition, some of the most economically important regions and cities in the world are vulnerable to storms and flooding and have been affected in recent years. These regions include the Gulf of Mexico and United States Gulf Coast, the US East Coast and New York City, the Philippines, Taiwan, Bangladesh, and Southeast Asia. Urban development in general is poor in some of these regions; in others, planning for storms and floods is only rudimentary. It seems impossible to limit growth in these areas without damaging the world economy, but millions of people are already at risk, and thousands more move to these regions every day.

Perspective One

In the past decade, major storms have damaged densely populated areas and killed thousands of people in Asia and the United States. Even though these areas are economically important, development must be curtailed in the interest of public safety. If slowing urban growth means limiting economic growth, so be it: the risks of flooding from unpredictable and violent climate patterns are too great.

Perspective Two

While it is true that a number of major industrial urban areas are located in areas vulnerable to storms and flooding in Asia and North America, development in these places must continue and industry must be fostered to ensure economic stability both locally and globally. Slowing business growth in these areas would irreparably damage the global financial and fossil fuel markets.

Perspective Three

Rapid economic growth is not at odds with smart urban development. Some of the most important economic and natural resources of the world are located in areas susceptible to storms and flooding; however, with the right planning and investment, economic growth can continue safely and affordably.

Sample Essay Response

It can certainly be argued that recent powerful and sometimes unexpected disruptive weather patterns and storms have caused extreme destruction. Furthermore, rapid population growth in areas vulnerable to storms and flooding puts millions at risk. Yet these growing centers of population are the economic engines of their economies and accommodate the workforces that drive the economic growth of these industrial powers. Development need not be curtailed in the interest of public safety. While adequate urban planning has not accompanied the rapid population growth, already with fatal consequences, it is not too late for safeguards to be put into place. Governments can still take steps to secure communities using lessons learned from past tragedies. While the risks of a calamitous storm should never be underestimated, the solution is not to halt migration and slow economic growth, but to encourage investment in urban planning and public safety.

Before growing urban areas get even larger, governments must take action to prevent the proliferation of slums, improve existing infrastructure to meet the needs of growing cities (or develop new infrastructure), and put policies into place for good urban management. In addition, given the importance of these urban and industrial areas, especially for billion-dollar sectors like oil and gas, there may even be opportunities for the private sector to get involved in sponsoring urban development and safety in the relevant economic zones and cities around the world.

The Gulf of Mexico and United States Gulf Coast are rich in oil and gas resources; moreover, Houston and New Orleans are major national and international ports. Securing the coastal areas is not only the right thing to do in order to save lives—it is a smart investment. Farther north, Hurricane Sandy hit New York City and the surrounding metro area. The seven million people in the region contribute to a cornerstone of the global economy; it is in the interest not only of the country but also of the world to protect their communities so that these workers can do their jobs and grow their families safely. Slowing business growth in these areas would damage the global financial and fossil fuel markets.

The fast-growing parts of South and Southeast Asia vulnerable to storms like the Philippines, Bangladesh, Myanmar, Vietnam, Malaysia, and Indonesia are home to the factories and the workers who produce many of the world's consumer products. Again, it is in the global interest to protect the local economies, which means protecting not just the industrial infrastructure but also the lives of the people there who work in that infrastructure. In addition, slowing development now because of environmental risk would destabilize these countries, and millions of poor and working-class people would suffer from job loss and lack of opportunities.

Innovation and technology accompany economic growth. Today, there are more opportunities than ever to develop products and procedures to ensure safety. Municipalities can establish evacuation routes and procedures; local authorities can be dispatched to provide assistance after a storm; and survival products such as water purifiers are available to the public. Civic organizations and NGOs distribute preparedness items during storm seasons, especially to those poor and working people who are the most likely to be affected or harmed. Technology and community coordination can ensure that vulnerable workers and their families are as safe as possible during storm season, so that they could benefit year-round from economic growth.

While storms and other natural disasters are and will remain a threat to human life, it is unrealistic to imagine that all economic activity will stop for the sake of safety. Thanks to economic growth and innovation, we can develop planning, technology, policy, and coordination to ensure the safety of communities as they drive the economic growth of those regions affected by major storms. That way, development can continue in as safe an environment as possible.

CPSIA information can be obtained
at www.ICGtesting.com
Printed in the USA
LVOW09s1330271217
560955LV00020B/127/P